WHAT PEOPLE ARE SAYING ABOUT

THE CAVEMAN RULES OF SURVIVAL

With the help of Dawn's online therapy, I learned that the little voice in my head was caused by "stuff" in my subconscious – stuff that I could reframe, so the voice didn't just quieten down but completely disappeared. I learned that my caveman brain was taking over and trying to keep me safe – and with the aid of Dawn's therapy sessions and downloads, I learned a new way of seeing the world... The lessons I've learned have changed my life, my career, my family – everything. If I could share one thing, it would be Dawn's message.
Rachel Lucas, Author

I enjoyed this book immensely; it offers sensible advice and says new things in an accessible way. All my research is geared towards helping us understand why we are as we are, and why we act the way we do, and *The Caveman Rules* clearly helps us to do those things. It could be as big as *Emotional intelligence*!
Trevor Harley, Professor of Psychology, Dundee University

The Caveman Rules of Survival

3 Simple Rules Used by Our Brains
to Keep Us Safe and Well

The Caveman Rules of Survival

3 Simple Rules Used by Our Brains
to Keep Us Safe and Well

Dawn C. Walton

CHANGE
MAKERS
BOOKS

Winchester, UK
Washington, USA

First published by Changemakers Books, 2014
Changemakers Books is an imprint of John Hunt Publishing Ltd., Laurel House, Station Approach,
Alresford, Hants, SO24 9JH, UK
office1@jhpbooks.net
www.johnhuntpublishing.com
www.changemakers-books.com

For distributor details and how to order please visit the 'Ordering' section on our website.

ISBN: 978 1 78279 757 9
Library of Congress Control Number: 2014946459

A CIP catalogue record for this book is available from the British Library.

Design: Lee Nash

Printed and bound by CPI Group (UK) Ltd, Croydon, CR0 4YY

We operate a distinctive and ethical publishing philosophy in all
areas of our business, from our global network of authors to
production and worldwide distribution.

CONTENTS

Foreword

My life was going brilliantly when I first spoke to Dawn Walton. I'd self-published my first novel, and watched it rise to the Amazon Top 10 within six weeks of publication. I'd signed with a major literary agency, was on the brink of agreeing a three book deal with Pan Macmillan, and I was a popular, outgoing member of the UK blogging community, talking regularly at conferences and giving workshops.

That was the theory, anyway...

In truth, I was in a perpetual state of panic that I was going to be found out. I'd be out there, selling myself as positive, confident and sociable, but inside there was a little voice nagging away telling me I wasn't good enough and didn't deserve any of this. I'd be telling people to get out, be positive, believe in themselves – and then I'd want to go home and hide under the blankets.

With the help of Dawn's online therapy, I learned that the little voice in my head was caused by "stuff" in my subconscious – stuff that I could reframe, so the voice didn't just quieten down but completely disappeared. I learned that my caveman brain was taking over and trying to keep me safe – and with the aid of Dawn's therapy sessions and downloads, I learned a new way of seeing the world.

Now, instead of feeling sick with nerves, I relish the challenge of standing up and talking at a conference. My writing career is soaring forwards because I've stopped subconsciously sabotaging myself. Even if I have a bad day – and we all do – I'm able to see it for what it is. It's just a bad day, not a sign that I'm a bad person, not a sign that I don't deserve happiness.

The lessons I've learned have changed my life, my career, my family – everything. If I could share one thing, it would be Dawn's message.

Read this book. Understand The Caveman Rules and every-thing in life will fall into place.

Rachael Lucas, Best Selling Author

Introduction

I sat in an old fashioned, slightly worn, armchair in a room in Harley Street. It struck me as out of place in such a prestigious location. I placed my legs and arms carefully in a relaxed pose in an attempt to hide my nerves. The room was quiet. I was sure the churning of my stomach, and the loud beating of my heart would give me away. Trevor, a Cognitive Hypnotherapist who I was there to see, sat just a few feet away in a similar granny-style armchair. I had been told he could help me in just a few sessions. I didn't believe it, but I did hope it was true. That is why I had jumped on a plane from a small airport in Dundee and flown to London. Apparently Trevor could use hypnosis to make me happy.

So why was I there if I was so sceptical? I wasn't sure. I asked myself that a lot in the days before my appointment. Like many people I wanted to believe in magic. I wanted to believe that I could get relief from the pain of memories and thoughts in my head. I wanted a reason to hope.

"How will you know what we do here today will have worked?" he asked with a kind voice.

This strange man was going to look in my head. All I wanted to do was run away.

"When my daughter asks me if I am happy, I don't want to have to lie to her," I answered.

He smiled.

We chatted some more. We had been talking on email for about a month before that first appointment, so he had a good idea of why I was there. He had explained why he believed he could help me. He explained the way the mind, and specifically memory, works. By the time I travelled to London I was beginning to believe he could help me.

"If you can just close your eyes."

Distracted by my attempts to appear calm despite the rising panic, I'd forgotten that bit. Hypnosis meant going into a trance and succumbing to the will of someone else. I shifted uncomfortably in my chair and resolved that, even though my eyes were closed, I would not do anything he told me to do. Yet, within seconds, a series of memories began to appear in my mind. "Am I making these up or are they real moments?" I wondered.

Soon I lost track of time as he guided me through my life to earlier memories. My position in the chair didn't matter anymore. My heartbeat settled as I became fully immersed in the movies behind the thoughts and feelings that had been painful for me for so long.

And then I was about six years old, standing outside the kitchen door with my older brother next to me. My stepmother stood in the doorway. She had just clouted me hard across the head. I was in shock. I was scared. I had a stain on my top, and it seemed that was the reason for getting hit. I could see and feel that moment as if it had happened the day before, not thirty-four years before.

The voice in the background, my guide, asked: "If she could learn something that would allow her to let go of the belief that there was something wrong with her, what might that be?"

"Duck and run!" I giggled. It seemed like really good advice.

Trevor didn't seem to agree. I was a little disappointed because I'd already imagined the look on my stepmother's face if I'd done that.

"What might have made her act in that way?" he asked.

"Dunno," I answered. It's hard when you are six to understand why adults behave in certain ways.

At this point he started to draw the adult me into this picture; the one sitting in Harley Street. He encouraged me to look, with adult eyes, at what it might be about my stepmother that made her behave in that way. He helped me see that she was angry and had her own issues. He helped me see that my brother was treated the same way. He helped me see that this wasn't about me; it was about her.

He asked me again what I could do to pass that lesson down to the younger version of me. This time I had a different idea. I crouched down next to her and explained about the caveman brain. I explained how we are programmed to do whatever is necessary to keep the bond strong with our parents. I explained that it was part of her programming to feel responsible, but it was not her fault that she was getting hit. This would be a useful lesson for her as she grew up. She could let go of the belief that she was broken and flawed. (I also told her to duck – it seemed a shame to miss that chance!)

Later that day I sat in London City airport waiting for my flight home. I became aware that something was missing. It took me a while to work out what was different. The voice was quiet. The voice, which I hadn't even realised was there until now, was silent. The voice that shouted "I hate you" constantly. The voice that talked about how useless I was and how I should not even try because there was no point. I was not good enough. "Give up," the voice would say. "You are broken". The voice was silent. I smiled. Maybe it was true? Maybe this guy had actually helped shift something already – in just one session.

Have you ever experienced a battle with yourself? An ongoing dialogue between a part of you that wants to do something and an inner voice that seems to be holding you back? In this book, I will explain how to identify the purpose of this inner voice, which I believe is trying to protect us from events that hurt us in childhood. I'll refer to these experiences as "Things." These "Things" are significant because they trigger a primal drive from our subconscious to protect us. I call it a "primal drive" because it is based on an outdated rule set from the caveman days.

I want to help you to see that clearing the Thing out of the way is not as difficult as you might think. In my experience, there is no problem that doesn't have, at its root, something that triggered a protective state in the subconscious during childhood. This might result in mental health conditions such as anxiety or depression. Or it could result in addictions such as food, gambling, alcohol, and drugs. It can even be the cause of stress-related physical illnesses such as Irritable Bowel and Chronic Fatigue Syndrome. I believe that behind all these conditions we can find a Thing which our subconscious is trying to protect us from.

There are three basic rules of survival used by your subconscious to keep you safe and alive. It is one or more of these rules that is usually the basis of you developing a Thing (or Things) that can get in the way of life when you are an adult. The reason that they can be so damaging and limiting is that these rules are based on the requirements to survive in the days when we were cavemen. Unfortunately it seems that they haven't really been updated through evolution to fit in with our modern society.

Rule Number 1 – React First or You'll Die!

This rule is about fear and how to respond when under threat. It is applied from the moment you are born. It is a fundamental and primitive principle, to already have the basic skills and capabilities necessary for survival at the moment of birth. As a result, this rule requires that when faced with something that will hurt you (these days emotionally or physically), then you must react instantly and instinctively. It is not conducive to survival to take time to think through various scenarios to find the optimum outcome.

Rule Number 2 – If Your Parents Don't Love You, You Will Die!

This rule is about understanding the impact that your actions and behaviours have on the bond with your parents. The desire to care for our young is a primitive one, but you can see many examples in the animal world where the bond is broken, or is never established, and the young animal dies. This was the same in the caveman days. This rule begins to kick in when you are capable of understanding different emotions and are able to equate your behaviours to the effect they have on the emotions of your parents.

Rule Number 3 – If You Are Not Part of a Pack, You Will Die!

This rule is about how you define your self-worth based on the people around you, and the role you play in society. Survival on your own, when you had to hunt and gather to live, was almost impossible, so we evolved to work together – to follow the strongest and to remove the weakest. This rule begins to kick in around the age of puberty, when your role in the pack changes from being a dependent one to a responsible one.

During my years as a Cognitive Hypnotherapist, when clients first come to see me, I have learnt to ask, "What's that about?" as they start to describe how their problem is getting in the way of their life. We are all unique, and labels are really only useful when you need to diagnose and come up with a medical solution. In my world, it doesn't really matter what the label for the problem is – anxiety, depression, overweight/underweight, self-esteem – whatever label the system would give them doesn't tell me anything useful when it comes to helping them. The way they "do" their problem will be unique to them, and that's what I need to work on. What I mean by "do" their problem is what thoughts and behaviours do they use to let them know they have a problem?

A fellow therapist once asked for ideas to help a client who was phobic of heights. The client was due to take a trip abroad, a journey which would require driving along high mountain roads. The thought of it terrified him. When my colleague tried to find the underlying cause of the phobia, she couldn't find anything. The client struggled to even recall a feeling strong enough for my fellow therapist to work with. I asked her a simple question: "How does he know he is scared of heights if he can't recall either an event or a feeling?" If the client could answer that question, then the therapist could find a route to a solution. In the end, the client knew he was scared of heights because of the physical anxiety he felt whenever he was high up. That was all she needed to help him change.

I approach each new client in the same way.

The first thing I need to do is to understand how you know you have a problem. This may sound like a weird thing to say, but there will be something about your behaviour that you want to lose. There will be something that motivated you to get in touch with me. You may have always had the problem, or it may be a recent thing, but at the end of the day you are unlikely to come to me just because you don't feel right. You are going to come and see me because your problem has started limiting your life. At some point, the fear of contacting a stranger for help becomes easier to overcome than coping with a problem day in, day out. For example:

She feels fat and unhealthy, which means that she doesn't feel comfortable in her clothes, and she shies away from activities that make her more self-aware, like swimming.

He can't seem to find the motivation to do anything.

She feels like there is no hope for the future, and so she is increasingly withdrawing from society.

He feels anxious, so he avoids situations which make the anxiety worse, like social interaction or speaking out for himself.

Limiting behaviour is not a conscious choice. It happens automatically in your subconscious. If you could consciously choose to do whatever you wanted to do, and be whoever you wanted to be, life would be a lot easier (and I'd be out of a job!).

The second thing I need to understand is how we will both know when you are no longer experiencing the problem. This needs to be clearly measurable. There needs to be a way to see evidence of change. It may seem that this is cut and dried when it comes to clients who want to lose weight, and harder with others, but even with weight loss clients, this can be tricky. If, for example, a client says she wants to lose weight for health reasons, then how will she know when she is healthier? Think about it. How do you define healthy? By what you eat? How much exercise you do? The type of exercise? Or maybe it's just the choice to walk instead of drive. The things we struggle with have a different meaning to each of us. So when I work with you on a problem, I also have to work with you on how you will know when our time together has made enough of a difference for you to be happy. This is the point at which I ask the magic wand question: "If I had a magic wand and I could wave it now, and you had achieved everything you wanted from working with me, how would you know?"

You see, the challenge in working with thoughts is that you can't see them. Thoughts are not tangible. This means that it can be easy to write off changes as coincidence unless you are primed to look for differences. Some people won't have any idea of where they want to get to. They just want to stop being where they are right now. That's okay. In itself that gives me a lot of information to work with. The important thing for both of us to understand is: "How will you know that what we've done has worked?" Sometimes the very act of answering that question helps us both achieve some level of clarity on what the real problem is.

Within the space of one session it is possible to see a significant difference in a client's thought process. However, because these changes can't be seen outwardly, they aren't clearly measurable. To help facilitate change, I need to prime my clients on how to see, experience and process the differences. I need to alert them to "the art of the possible", where even one small difference is enough to establish evidence of wider changes to come. If I am too prescriptive, then it's possible that my clients will overlook differences that may be unexpected. To get around this, I try to open up their minds to what might change in as generic a way as possible, by using vague language like "things" and "stuff". This allows their mind to replace those words with specific ones that are unique to them.

Finally, once I know the problem and how we will measure change, it is time for me to get rid of it. Everyone has a "Thing" – the thing that the subconscious is using to trigger a behaviour pattern. My job is to find the Thing and clear it out of the way. This can be an evolutionary process, with each session giving you more and more clarity about who you will be once you are free of your problem. It's a fun process (well, for me anyway) that can be likened to watching a butterfly learning how to flap its wings. There is no better feeling than seeing a client free to fly away and get on with their life.

You might find that, as you read through this book, a lot of examples in your own life start coming to mind that begin to make a lot more sense than they ever have. That's a good thing. You might find that understanding the common root causes of different behaviours is all you need to clear it out of the way. If not, find someone to help!

The Subconscious and the Rulebook

Are you scared of spiders? If you're not, I bet you know someone who is. In the UK the top two phobias are spiders and snakes. The irony of this is that there are no venomous spiders in the UK and almost no snakes. Most people will never see a snake in the wild in their lifetime. Now think about the situation in which someone is scared of spiders. Is his behaviour normal? Is that person, when in fear, the same as he is when he is not in fear? A friend once described his male friend as being "a big girl" because when he saw a spider, he freaked. Clearly he was not himself. He was under the control of his subconscious, which is the part of the brain that is not rational; it is emotional and responsible for keeping you safe from harm. That part of his brain saw the spider as a threat. This altered state is typically referred to as a trance state by hypnotherapists and psychologists. This seemingly strong and together male lost it when confronted with a tiny creature that can easily be squished with a boot. If only fear was a rational thing!

The reality is, whenever you are behaving in a way you would consciously choose not to, then you are in a trance state (i.e., your subconscious is in control). Have you ever driven through a set of traffic lights only to wonder if the light was actually on green? Trance. Have you ever walked out of your front door only to get halfway down the street and wonder if you really locked it? Trance.

It's been said your subconscious is in charge for 90% of the day. Actually, some say that it's in control for 95% of the day, but I find it hard to believe we have so little control, even though I know it may well be right. Anyway I guess 5% is neither here nor there in the grand scheme of things. The point is that you are not the boss of you; your subconscious is. I suppose if that's the way it's meant to be, then there really shouldn't be a problem.

However, let's consider for a moment the role of your subconscious. It's pretty simple really. The role of the subconscious is to do whatever is necessary to protect you and keep you alive. It is a primitive and emotional part of your brain, which is a bit of a problem when you consider how much of the time it is the boss of your actions!

Consider for a moment the difference between animals and humans. Animals are driven by their basic instincts. These can be summed up simply as eating and procreating. Everything in between is about recovery from those two things. Animals don't think and analyse stuff because they don't need to. They exist, and they react, and they stay alive and safe to the best of their abilities in the environment in which they live. An animal doesn't need a purpose or a reason to exist. They just live in the moment. If you were to put a wild animal in a situation where there was plenty of food, most wouldn't store it. (Those that do only do it for the purpose of hibernation.) Food is for eating. They don't need the ability to resist their primitive needs because that adds nothing to their chances for survival.

In many ways, your brain is very similar to the animal brain. Your subconscious can be compared to the core brain function of an animal. It is also driven by basic primitive needs. It too is designed to respond based on instinct instead of calculated thought. Remember, this is the part of your brain that is in charge for 90% of the day. Most of your day you are driven by thoughts and behaviours based on a primitive need to survive. You might refer to this as instinct. You respond to most of what happens based on instinct. You form an opinion of someone in the first few seconds. For all the weighing up of pros and cons, most of us make big decisions based on what feels right. We are creatures driven by instinct and feelings who believe we are driven by logic.

It's probably easy to accept the automatic functions of the subconscious: the part that keeps your heart pumping, your lungs breathing and all other ongoing bodily functions that keep you alive. It can be a bit more of a stretch to realise that also in that 90% are semi-automatic functions. Have you ever been on a journey and reached your destination only to realise that you don't actually remember anything about the actual journey itself? If so, then you know how easy it is to go into this semi-automatic state. This can be even more worrying when it's a road trip and you were the driver! Some people might call this daydreaming. You are daydreaming for far more of the time than you realise.

When something happens to a person that damages their brain, like a stroke, you become more aware of the importance of those semi-automatic functions. Losing the ability to do something simple that you always took for granted, like lifting a cup to your lips, shows how much of what you do is actually semi-automatic.

Think about breathing. Breathing will happen naturally without any intervention, but you can consciously focus on, and take control of, your breathing. Slow down each breath in and each breath out. Breathe in for a different count than breathing out. You can consciously take control of your breathing, or you can forget about it and allow your subconscious to manage the whole process. You can't, however, hold your breath until you die. Your subconscious simply won't let you. (Please don't try and test that so that you can prove me wrong!)

The thoughts that flow around your head are similar to breathing. A whole bunch of stuff happens automatically. Even more happens semi-automatically. You know how to put on jeans or a shirt without having to give it any conscious thought until you are drunk or over-tired, when everything seems to require more of a conscious effort. Unless you have experienced any sort of brain damage, you can walk without having to think about it. When you run, most of you will have to be more consciously aware of your pace and foot placement. Sitting watching TV, only a small part of you will be paying attention to what you are watching, while at the same time other thoughts about things you need to do or what has happened in your day will be flying around. You might even find that things on the TV are triggering memories and emotions that are stored in your subconscious somewhere.

When I was a child I read Roald Dahl's *The Wonderful Story of Henry Sugar*. Most people haven't heard of this particular book, but it fascinated me because in it there was a character who could look at a room and memorise enough in a few seconds to navigate around the room with his eyes closed. He trained himself to do this by looking at the flame on a candle and then closing his eyes and holding the image of the flame in his mind for as long as possible. For years after I was obsessed with doing this (and I still am to some degree), but I have never managed to do it for more than a couple of seconds. My mind is simply too active with all its different thoughts. Try it. You might be surprised at how difficult it is. This practice would be referred to as mindfulness these days. Mindfulness is great for both physical and mental rejuvenation and can be very effective at allowing you to make the most of the 10% and quieten down some of the more negative thoughts that happen in the remaining 90%. We'll look at this more at the end of this book.

You can, and do, function perfectly well with your subconscious being in the driving seat. That is, you do until that part of you kicks into protection overdrive for some unknown reason. Then it can really begin to get in the way of your life. You see, given that it is so primitive and so emotional, it is very easy for the subconscious part of your brain to make a miscalculation about something that is going to harm you. Let me give you an example from when I was a child:

My mother was very much into horses, so I used to go out riding with her to keep her company. I hated horses, to be honest, but I was a child, so I didn't really have a choice in the matter. Horses don't deal very well with unfamiliar stuff; if they ride the same route day in day out they are particularly sensitive to new items appearing on that route. A horse needs time to process. It needs to stop and look and make sure something is safe. If you don't give it that time, then there is a high probability that it will spook and run away if it spots something unfamiliar. On this particular day, someone had left a blue plastic bag by the side of the road. Clearly this had not been there before, and my horse decided that this was a threat. To my horse a blue plastic bag fluttering in the breeze was unknown and therefore a risk; it was potentially something that could cause harm, like a predator. The way horses deal with predators is to run, and it didn't matter that it had a person on its back! Off we set, and despite me heaving on the reins, the brakes just weren't working. Once sufficiently clear of the threat, my horse decided to slam the brakes on and stopped dead. The inevitable consequence was that I went flying over its neck and landed on the ground with a thump. Luckily nothing was broken. The blue plastic bag triggered a flight response in my horse. It was pure protection from a perceived threat.

All through your life you encounter metaphorical blue plastic bags. These are triggers that set off a protection response in your subconscious. A protection response is one where your subconscious shuts off your ability to think rationally and acts on the basis of The Caveman Rules of Survival. Once a trigger has been activated, unless you respond to it with the appropriate flight, fight, freeze response, then your subconscious will continue to escalate the response until you listen. If you do respond appropriately (according to whatever rule of survival your subconscious is following), by giving in to the fight, flight, freeze response, then you are stuck with that response for the rest of your life. This is because your subconscious has been validated and will continue to trigger the same response even at the thought of the trigger being present in your future. It is impossible to un-see something you have seen. This means that once a protection response has been activated in the subconscious, it will continue to attempt to protect you whenever it perceives a threat from that trigger. However, it will also gradually expand the scope to include more and more similar situations until soon, things that used to be perfectly fine for you, now trigger an anxiety-based reaction. The only way to change it is to get rid of the Thing that triggered the response in the first place. It's easier to understand this in animals but maybe a little trickier to see a situation where you are terrified of standing up and talking to a room full of people in the same way. When I go into the first caveman rule of survival in more detail in the next chapter, hopefully it will begin to make more sense.

The problem is that we all have our own unique triggers. These triggers become rules for survival that are written into your own personal rulebook all through childhood. This rulebook is then followed once you are an adult and no longer under the protection of your parents. This is why you can find yourself reacting badly to something, while everyone else around you seems to be fine. It simply means that particular rule doesn't exist in anyone else's rulebook.

Another thing I have observed when working with clients is that people have a tendency to compare themselves to other people. The problem with this is that you often perceive that everyone else is okay and you are the one who is different and messed up. Most people don't realise that we all have our own rulebooks and therefore our own issues. Just because a person isn't running out of the room screaming doesn't mean that she isn't also fighting a battle inside her head with a voice that's saying things like: "You aren't good enough", "You don't fit in", "Everyone is looking at you", "Get out of here before you look stupid like you always do." Everybody has a voice inside of them that is trying to protect them. That voice, believe it or not, is actually designed to protect you from getting into situations that might hurt you.

The biggest shift that I often see when working with a client is when they begin to understand that the internal battle is normal; the voice they hear doesn't necessarily speak the truth – it's just a matter of perception. For example, for clients that thinks everyone is judging them, I usually set them a task to find one instance in every day where they think that their actions or thoughts have annoyed or upset someone. (This is usually very easy.) Then I ask them to think, "*If* this was not about me but about something to do with the other person, what *might* it be about?" They don't have to believe it's true. They just need to shift their perceptual position for a moment and realise that we all have another voice in our heads. It's amazing how quickly this can become a habit, rather than a task. They get so caught up in their own stuff, they don't realise that no one really cares what they are up to. We are all caught up in the daily dialogue between the protective voice in our head and the conscious choice to do what we want. It's quite a fun thing to do actually. You become a cross between a detective and a psychologist, and pretty soon it becomes really obvious that everyone has a rulebook with some interesting rules in it. We are all screwed up to some degree!

The New Kid on the Block

If the subconscious is in control for so much of that time, what is it that allows you to exert free will and choice over your behaviours? What stops you just eating and having sex all day (apart from when you are on honeymoon maybe!)?

The new kid on the block in the brain world is the prefrontal cortex. This is the part of the brain that separates you from animals, and is the part of your brain where self-control sits. Animals don't generally have this part, and the ones that do (apes, dolphins, and elephants to name a few) have a smaller version. In this situation, bigger is better because a bigger prefrontal cortex allows for more complex computation. I always think of this as the front part of your head – basically because that is where it is! This is where conscious rational thought comes from. As a relatively recent addition to your brain, it is pretty low down the pecking order. It is a non-critical part of the brain. Some people refer to it as completing executive functions because of this.

When engaged, this part of the brain allows you to make logical and rational choices over what you do in your day. It allows you to override an emotional reaction to something; on the basis that it is something you want to do. It is the prefrontal cortex and conscious thought, for example, that allows you to resist the call of the sweet or fatty food because you know it is not good for your health. It is your subconscious that can drag you back and make you eat it because of some emotional and primitive need for protection.

Let's consider an example:

As a child you were constantly told you were stupid. You decided you must be a horrible person that no one could possibly like.

It hurts to believe that you have such a hateful personality that not even your parents could love you. (You will read later how important it is to have the love of your parents.)

Your subconscious wants to keep you safe from being hurt, but how can it protect you from your own personality? It can't. Instead it can stop people getting close enough to get to know you.

Your subconscious determines that the best way to keep people at arm's length is to make you ugly. It can't change your genetic features, but it can make you fat so that your shape can not be discerned. Your subconscious drives you to gain weight.

You feel everyone hates you because you are fat and ugly, but somehow that is easier to accept than people hating you because you are not a nice person. At least you can lose weight – if you want to.

The irony is that you will probably be really miserable, because consciously you don't want to be overweight. However, your subconscious feels that to stop you being miserable it needs to keep the weight on.

We all have a battle going on between the different parts of our brain. The problem is that the rational part of our brain is only engaged for around 10% of the day. If there is something going on that triggers a subconscious protection response, then pretty much all of that 10% will be occupied by battling the 90% that is controlled by the subconscious. When all is equal, and there is no reason for protection, you can spend your 10% making the choices you want; choosing to do things that are important to you and your future. Your ability to look at things that deliver long term benefit, rather than instant gratification, is dependent on moving beyond primal needs. The prefrontal cortex allows you to make decisions based on weighing up alternatives and looking at longer term consequences. This is something animals (and younger children!) are incapable of because they depend on gut instinct.

The problem is, even your decision making is, in part, influenced by gut feelings otherwise known as instinct. One of the reasons humans struggle so hard to set, and stick to, long term goals is that we respond so much to the feedback we get in the moment about how things make us feel. Long term goals sit in that 10% of your thought process which means that they are beyond the rules of survival and gut instinct. If these goals are too abstract to keep your focus, when faced with a choice between instant gain and long term greater gain, you will often choose the smaller, more instant gain.

Because the prefrontal cortex is non-critical to survival and because it is a relatively new function of the brain, the subconscious has priority over conscious thought. Have you ever noticed how, when you are tired, you struggle to think straight? It's harder to make a simple choice, and you might even find that you get overly emotional for no obvious reason. Think of it like a car. If the battery is running a bit low, you don't switch the radio on. If you are running low on energy in your body, or if you are under what your subconscious perceives as a significant threat, then your prefrontal cortex, and thereby your self-control and decision making, gets switched off. The problem then is you are back to depending on your animal brain, and you can do crazy things like put a DVD you have just bought in the fridge! On one occasion, when this happened to me, I thought I'd lost it. It took me the whole day to realise that I'd actually put it in the fridge for some unknown reason. I was tired and hormonal because I was pregnant. Well, that's my excuse anyway! Whichever way you look at it, it is a fact that the prefrontal cortex needs energy to function. If you are tired, or your blood sugar is low, or you are exhausted because of stress or some other reason, then you default to your emotional brain – your survival brain. This gives the subconscious carte blanche to do whatever is necessary to keep you alive, and that is a very primitive approach.

By some miracle we seem to function perfectly well with the subconscious managing all the automatic and semi-automatic functions and the conscious part making plans, enjoying the moment and taking control. We don't even need to think about there being multiple voices having a constant internal dialogue. Most of the time the internal dialogue is not limiting what we want to do, and our brain performs nicely in harmony with the body. It is only when there is something getting in the way of our ability to make a free choice that we become aware of a battle with another part. In fact, even when the battle is in full force, we still tend to beat ourselves up for things we "should be able to do" or "shouldn't be doing". We find it hard to understand why we can't just get over stuff in the way that people around us seem to do so effortlessly.

The Subconscious is Like a Petulant Child

I find it easiest to think of the subconscious like a petulant child. What it wants, it gets, and if you try to say no, it throws a tantrum. The less you give in, the bigger the tantrum gets. When your subconscious is having a tantrum, it is almost impossible to focus on anything else. No matter how hard you try, your attention keeps getting drawn back to the same thing. Sometimes you find it easier to just give in to the inevitable and let your subconscious have its own way.

Can you think of the last time you tried to resist something you really wanted but knew was bad for you? Let's use chocolate as an example. Have you ever noticed how the more you try not to think of the chocolate, the more obsessed you seem to become? What if you got something more than taste from eating chocolate? Maybe it gives you comfort or makes you feel happy because it's a treat. Because the subconscious is so primitive, it might equate that feeling of comfort or happiness as also stopping you from feeling hurt. If it stops you from being hurt, it also means it keeps you safe and well. Basically, as far as your subconscious is concerned, if you don't have that chocolate, you are going to die! Putting it that way, then you can see that you would be crazy not to eat the chocolate. If you consider the chocolate as something you need for survival rather than just a nice taste, then it is easier to understand how your subconscious makes it impossible to resist. At the end of the day, if there is a part of you that believes that avoiding the chocolate is going to result in your death, then at some point you will have to give in to the inevitable and eat it. It is all a battle – a battle between the voice of self-control and the louder, more insistent voice that looks after your survival based on The Caveman Rules.

The thing is, your subconscious means well. Its intent is always to protect you. It's just unfortunate that, due to its primitive nature, the things it does to protect you often lead to the thing it's trying to protect you from. In trying to stop you being hurt, the behaviours you often end up exhibiting can be life-limiting and hurtful.

For example, imagine as a child you had a teacher that was a bit of a bully (not hard to imagine for most of us). She would pick on you to answer questions in class even though she knew you probably wouldn't know the answer making you feel stupid in front of the whole class (triggering Caveman Rule Number 3 about being the weakest in a pack). Your subconscious doesn't want you to feel stupid because it hurts – and just because it hurts you emotionally doesn't make it any less relevant – so a rule to protect you from that is established. The rule might read something like, "Don't do anything where people might spot that you are stupid because it hurts". As you grow up you become an underachiever because you avoid putting effort into anything you do. It's too risky. You avoid doing anything in work which will draw attention to you, because if you do something and you fail, then it's going to hurt. As a result you feel like you are stupid. You see other people around you achieving, and you know you could be just as good as them, if only you put the effort in, but that is just too much of a risk to take. The very thing your subconscious is trying to protect you from – feeling stupid – is the very thing that ends up happening.

This battle between protection and living your life with the freedom to exert self-control goes on all day every day. It may not always be obvious what you are battling. If you are struggling to stop smoking, then it's a little easier to accept that no matter how hard you try, you might end up giving in and having another cigarette. Smoking is an addiction, so you have an excuse. But what about feeling like you are useless and everyone hates you? What possible positive or protective intent could your subconscious have for making you believe that you are not good enough?

Believe it or not, issues of self-esteem and lack of confidence still come down to a subconscious drive to protect you from getting hurt. While we are all different, a common theme I find amongst my clients is the element of risk. At some point in your childhood, something has happened that hurt you emotionally. In this situation, the part of you that was trying to protect you decided that the best way to stop you getting hurt in the future was to get you to lie low. If you stick your head above the parapet, if you get noticed, then the risk of being hurt again significantly increases. So a rule is established to keep you in the background. Any time you try to do something that requires stepping out of your comfort zone or standing up for yourself, it fires off the trigger to access the rule. Initially this process begins with a feeling, or maybe just a second voice in your head; a voice that tells you that you are stupid to try something, that everyone else will be judging you. The voice may sound like it's mean and horrible, but actually all it's doing is trying to prevent you from taking action by making you doubt yourself. This voice is being cruel to be kind – it thinks!

If the first line of defence doesn't work, then the backup plan kicks in: a physical response. If you fail to listen to the warning voice when your subconscious believes you are at risk, it will use your body to hold you back. This can be just low level symptoms of anxiety, or if you stubbornly ignore it, can escalate into a full-blown panic attack. It can also result in a more subtle physical response that happens over time. The more you attempt to ignore the need for protection, the more your mind will use your body to put barriers in the way. Just because it is your head creating them does not make them any less real. These are very real physical symptoms including stomach problems, pain and lethargy. There is nothing your subconscious won't do to protect you from being hurt. It will always win eventually because survival trumps choice and rational thought. It believes that it is stopping you getting eaten by the sabre-toothed tiger, so in the end it is going to get its own way, whatever the day-to-day cost to you.

Writing the Rulebook

At this point you might wonder why some people go into this protection mode in some situations, when others are perfectly fine?

Let's look at the case of two eight-year-old twins. Both twins have a part in the school concert and will perform individually. The first twin walks onto the stage and trips, flailing his arms in a comedy stumble. The audience laughs. This first twin looks out and is mortified that everyone is laughing at him. He resolves never to do anything in public again and risk this bad feeling.

The second twin walks onto the stage and funnily enough trips in the same way as the other, also flailing his arms in a comedy stumble. The audience laughs once more. This twin, however, looks out on the laughing faces and thinks it's great. He resolves to do as much as he can in the future to make people laugh because it makes him feel so good.

What is the difference between the two twins? No idea. This is the problem. We have no idea what will become something that is significant to the subconscious and what won't.

What I do know, from working with clients, is that all through childhood the subconscious is writing rules into a rulebook. This rulebook is filled with instructions and guidelines for surviving, based on events and triggers that your subconscious has tagged as either a threat or something that hurts. It fills up pretty quickly with all sorts of different rules, things that will help with survival once you are no longer under the care and protection of your parents.

In my experience, once you reach the age of about 14-16, instead of writing rules in the rulebook, your subconscious begins to follow them. This is because, by then, you are on your own. It's the decisions that you make that determine your safety and wellbeing, not the decisions and guidance of your parents.

Like with any reference book, it is entirely possible that you can go through your whole life without even turning to a particular page. Sometimes people come to see me because something that has always been fine for them is increasingly becoming a problem. An event has caused their subconscious to turn to a new page with a previously unseen rule on it. Once the rule has been accessed, it is then applied from that point forward, and often situations that used to be perfectly okay become affected by this rule. You can't un-see something you've seen.

In later chapters I will explain the basis of some of these rules, but for now let me give you a few examples of the sorts of rules I have come across with my clients. With each of these rules, the client tends to struggle more with the fact that they don't understand why she reacts so strongly rather than with the actual behaviour itself. Once you can understand the rule underlying it, and the fact that the subconscious is just trying to protect you, then it can be easier to accept the behaviour.

Presenting problem: *You are too scared to speak out for yourself and shy away from confrontation.*
Rule: Because your father didn't listen to you, then you must not be worth listening to.
What your subconscious thinks is happening: To stop getting hurt, because you think your opinion doesn't count, you should stay away from offering your opinion.
The result: You shy away from offering a different opinion to others even though what they are saying can make you frustrated and angry. This often means that it feels like people walk all over you, leaving you feeling hurt and undervalued.

Presenting problem: *You want to lose weight.*
Rule: Your grandmother loved you because she always bought you sweets when you went to visit.
What your subconscious thinks is happening: Having sweets is a sign that you are loved, and if you are loved then you are cared for. It's a good thing, therefore, for you to eat sweet things.
The result: You can't resist sweet things. It makes you feel good to eat them even though afterwards you feel terrible about yourself because you are putting weight on. The good feeling is a short term gain while longer term you feel unlovable because you are overweight.

Presenting problem: *You have anxiety over social situations.*
Rule: Your first day at high school was scary. You didn't know anyone and were worried about being alone. You felt no one liked you.
What your subconscious thinks is happening: It was not a good feeling going into a situation with people you don't know so you should avoid that in the future.
The result: Since it is normal that you deal with the unknown all day every day, you never know what is going to happen. The anxiety gets rolled into a fear of the unknown and increases to the point where it becomes life-limiting. In attempting to protect you from being hurt, you end up believing there is something wrong with you because you are "no good around people".

Presenting problem: *You expect relationships to fail.*
Rule: You were bullied at school and cut out of the gang which hurt.
What your subconscious thinks is happening: You should protect yourself from getting hurt by not getting close to anyone.
The result: Because you assume that people are going to have

a problem with you, you push them away, protecting yourself from anyone getting close. The result is that you end up in a self-fulfilling prophecy alone because you push people away, thus proving that you can't be loved/liked, and you feel hurt.

These are just a few examples from clients of the sort of rules your subconscious might be following based on simple events in childhood. The problem is, you can never know which situations the subconscious will deem as significant enough for a rule, and which ones become just memories. Invariably when I guide my clients to find the moment that created a rule, I come across something that they didn't expect to be there. However, at the same time, they are surprised at how well they remember it as they look back. "I remember that moment", they say after, "but I didn't think it was a big enough deal to cause me a problem." Clearly though, the subconscious thought it was a big deal. It was significant enough to need a rule in the rulebook to protect them later on in life. This is a bit different from Freud's theories about stuff being buried deep; if it was buried that far down, it wouldn't be affecting your daily behaviour.

Later in this book we will look in more detail at how rules are established. For now, let's focus on how easy it is for a miscalculation to happen. How do relatively insignificant moments end up being regarded as significant enough to create a rule for survival?

Child vs Adult Understanding

The catch with the rulebook theory is that the rules are being written at a time where you have a limited ability to understand everything that is going on. It's almost like children see things with a cardboard box on their head with eye holes cut out! They simply cannot see everything that is going on around them. Children develop more complex reasoning and understanding as they get older. The establishment of rules is not about age or knowledge but about the technicalities of brain development. As I have said, in my experience, the rules are getting written in the rulebook anywhere up until the age of 14-16 at a time when the brain is still developing. From that point forward, the rules are being followed instead of written. The earlier it is when a rule gets put into the rulebook, the more significant the miscalculation is likely to be. Conclusions are being reached on what stuff means, and what your subconscious needs to protect you from, with this limited understanding.

I once had a manager who refused to see anyone else's point of view. It was really a challenge because you couldn't reason with him. It was almost at a level where I wanted to scream with frustration. I would say a pen was red, and he'd say, "No it's black." I'd say, "It's red because your tie is also red," and he'd answer, "The tie is not relevant to the argument." (Obviously we weren't talking about the colour of a pen, but you get the idea.) The subconscious is very much like this.

There are numerous studies into childhood cognitive reasoning and most have evolved into theories of development. These theories tend to be angled towards the area of interest of the person doing the studying. Freud was a bit obsessed with sexual development. Erik Eriksson took Freud's work and looked at social development. Piaget tended to be the one who looked at it from a reasoning point of view (also Vygotsky, who looked at things in a similar way).

For now, let me focus on Piaget and, rather than make this chapter a compare and contrast of different development phases in children, I will use his ideas to map onto the role that The Caveman Rules play as a child develops. Piaget outlined three stages of child development. The first he called the sensorimotor stage which is all about the ability to understand about objects: to know that they exist, even without you being able to see them, and to understand that an object is the same even if the size is changed by distance and perspective, etc. According to Piaget this stage is applicable between the ages of 0-2 years old. In terms of The Caveman Rules, this does not really play a part in the processing of rules into the rulebook. What is relevant, though, is that rules that are written at a very early age tend to have a more profound effect on our adult life. It has even been known for things that happen in the womb to trigger a protective behaviour in later life, although in my experience, most clients have rules going into their rulebook from about six months onwards.

The next stage tends to have more relevance to the rulebook. Piaget called this the concrete operations stage or the age of curiosity. This is the age between two and eleven, which is really a big span if you consider all the development changes that happen in the early years. According to Piaget this is where the child is learning the relationship between objects, for example, one pencil is longer than another, one box is bigger than another, etc. Younger children can still struggle with applying reasoning to that. So for example, having learnt the rule that boxes are blue, when presented with a purple box they may not see it as a box because it's not blue like the first one.

This difficulty with reasoning can lead to miscalculations in the significance of events. I suspect this limitation in development is the reason why the most significant miscalculations I see in clients tend to happen before the age of eleven. While Piaget theorised that the threshold between this and the next stage was around eleven, he did not really believe in a particularly scientific approach to his work, so I suspect there is wiggle room in the age brackets!

I have a friend whose three-year-old daughter occasionally gets taken to bed by her grandma. Her grandma reads her a story but always has to get her glasses first. "I have to get my glasses so I can read," she tells the little girl. Then one day the little girl asks her mother, "Mummy, when will I be old enough to get those glasses that mean I can read?" It's a simple miscalculation based on limited understanding.

To expand on this, there was an experiment done with five-year-old children. A child was sat on either side of a screen so that they could hear but not see each other. One child was asked to describe an object they had to the other child. They failed to do this because they have no concept of other people having a different way of thinking. As far as they are concerned, whatever makes sense to them also makes sense to everyone else.

Now take a five-year-old and put her in a situation where her teacher shouts at her and she runs away because she's scared. She gets in even more trouble because she has run away, and the whole thing gets blown out of proportion to the degree where, in adult life, any sort of confrontation triggers an anxiety response. The more the adult tries to resist and get on with her life, the more the subconscious tries to pull her back. Eventually all it takes is for someone to offer a different opinion for a panic attack to get triggered. All this because at five years old this child felt that the teacher was cross at *her*, which resulted in a rule going into the rulebook as follows:

It hurts when someone shouts at you; if you detect confrontation, engage flight mode.

When able to look back on that scene through adult eyes, it becomes clear that the teacher shouted at everyone, not just her. It is clear that she had actually told her mum how scared she was, but her mum hadn't listened. It is clear that it wasn't about her but about the adults around her. All the subconscious needed was to be shown that, and the rule becomes unnecessary.

It's amazing what you miss when you are looking on the world with such limited understanding (back to the cardboard box on the head image!). You think you are seeing everything that goes on, but you are really only seeing within the confines of the box. A lot of my work involves lifting the metaphorical box off the head of a younger version of the client allowing her to see what was going on around her with adult eyes.

The third stage in Piaget's model is the formal operations stage where a child develops mental reasoning and a value system. According to Piaget, this happens after eleven. In some ways it is trickier once you are between the ages of 11-16. Your subconscious is still making the same miscalculations, but now it's doing it based on far more subtle events. Instead of needing to be directly shouted at to know you have done wrong, you are able to interpret moods and different behaviours. You still believe, because of the cardboard box on your head, that everything is about you, but the scope for what might now translate into a rule in your rulebook becomes so much wider.

For example, imagine you ran a race at eight years old, and you came second in the race. Given your limited understanding, you might decide that it sucks to not win at stuff and that actually the best way to avoid that feeling is to avoid competitive stuff when you are older. Because of your box, what you might not realise is that the reason you lost was because you had a big breakfast that morning and were feeling a bit sick. Or maybe the person who beat you actually went on to win a whole series of races at quite a high level. Because of the cardboard box on your head, you might only remember that you did or didn't do something and it didn't feel good and not realise there were valid reasons behind that event not working out so well.

Now let's look at how this kind of limitation can get in the way of your life. You are thirteen years old and your mother asks your opinion on the dress she is wearing. You tell her you don't like it, and she bursts into tears. She cries for a long time and then spends the next day or two barely talking to you. You feel guilty. You've made your mum cry. Maybe you shouldn't have said what you thought. Maybe a rule needs to go into the rulebook to protect you in the future that says, "Keep your opinions to yourself." Once you are an adult, as you look back on that moment you realise your mother must have been going through a really rough patch when the opinion of her thirteen-year-old daughter could send her into such a low mood. How low must her self-esteem have been for it to affect her that much? And you can even take this further and say how inappropriate it was for her to even ask for her daughter's opinion and how unfair to then treat her so badly for answering. Without the cardboard box on your head, you can see there is a lot more going on here. It can give things that happen when you were a child a whole new perspective. The thing is, while that moment was clearly significant, you may not have given it a second thought at any point in your adult life. With hindsight and the ability to look back on moments that your subconscious treats as significant, it becomes blatantly obvious how easy it is for miscalculations to happen.

Generally, you are writing the rules in your rulebook up until the age of fourteen (although I have had a few examples where the rules came about when the client was sixteen). Even though the textbooks say that you are stuck on nominal processing until about the age of ten, it is my experience that these miscalculations can continue to happen until the age of sixteen. Basically, all the time your caveman brain believes you are dependent on someone for survival, it is important for it to be calculating what moments mean and keeping track of rules for use in later life.

So what is the subconscious watching out for? In the absence of sabre-toothed tigers or any form of predator, how does your subconscious decide what is a threat to your survival and what is a meaningless event? This is where the three caveman rules of survival come in.

Caveman Rule Number 1 – React First or You'll Die!

You are a caveman out on your daily hunt. These hunts don't happen often, and anything you catch will keep you going for the next few weeks (not that you have an idea what a week is). You have become separated from the other cavemen mid-hunt and are trying to find your way back to the pack.

As you come around a big rock, you notice a sabre-toothed tiger staring at you. It licks its lips. It looks like today is its lucky day. If you were a modern-day human with a shiny prefrontal cortex that allows you to consider all the different possibilities and outcomes of this interaction, you might find you have a bit of a problem. By the time you have thought, "Hmm, is this my best spear? Can I outrun the tiger on this terrain?", you would probably find the sabre-toothed tiger, unburdened by the need to evaluate all options, has closed the gap between you and is now chewing on your leg.

Luckily, in the caveman days your prefrontal cortex is not fully developed, and instead your emotional brain is in charge. Your subconscious will take control of this situation. The most important thing to do to increase your chance of survival is to respond instantly – to get your body ready to react as quickly as possible.

Fight, Flight, Freeze

The first thing that is triggered by your subconscious is a release of adrenaline. Adrenaline is a hormone secreted by the adrenal glands when you are under stress. As the adrenaline takes over your body, a number of things happen:

1. Most viruses in the body run away and hide. Adrenaline is like a super bug, and nothing else has a chance while it is

around. Think about it. It really wouldn't be much good for survival if you were going, "Oooh, I can't fight you today I'm afraid; I have a really bad flu and feel like I'm dying. Just eat me and put me out of my misery." Have you ever noticed when you are working in a highly stressful role that whenever you take time off work, the first thing that happens is that you get ill? This is because, under stress, your body is constantly flooded with adrenaline, so the other bugs are being suppressed. The minute you start to relax, the adrenaline leaves your body, and the bugs take the chance to have their say.

2. A physical change happens. Your heart rate increases as blood begins to pump around your body faster. Your breath gets shorter. You are now on a heightened state of alert. Your body is ready to react in the most appropriate way to the threat of the sabre-toothed tiger. What the most appropriate response is will very much depend on your experience of similar situations or whatever your caveman dad taught you. There are three different responses that this heightened state of alert is getting you ready for.

Flight

Get ready to run away as fast as you can. Thanks to your subconscious, your body is primed to escape at the fastest possible speed. I am sure you have read of feats of amazing strength under extremely difficult circumstances, or even experienced times yourself where you just coped and then afterwards, when you looked back, you even amazed yourself by what you had done.

Fight

It may be that outrunning the sabre-toothed tiger is just not an option. In this case the adrenaline coursing through your body should give you the strength and courage to face the tiger. In the cold light of day, no one in their right mind would take on the tiger, but once your subconscious has worked its magic, you are good to go. The adrenaline running through your body will give you the added bonus of instinctive responses and also the ability to ignore the pain from being clawed or bitten. After all, stopping and going, "Ouch, ouch, ouch that hurt!" is only going to end badly. My husband once told me the story of when he crashed his motorbike. His little finger was hanging on by a thread, but far from screaming in agony he happily took the offer of a cup of a tea from a kind lady who lived close by. Even though he was drinking the tea with his finger hanging off, the scale of what had happened did not hit him until later.

Freeze

This one is often overlooked in what is referred to as a fight or flight response. I am sure you can all think of times where you were hiding and it felt like your heart was beating so loudly that it would surely give you away. Many animals use freezing as a very effective way of avoiding getting eaten. Believe it or not, the adrenaline flooding your body gives you a heightened control over your body, allowing you to freeze more effectively.

With your body now flooded with adrenaline, your mind is now exclusively focussed on instinctive response. It is said strong emotion makes you stupid because in a heightened emotional state such as fear, your prefrontal cortex is switched off. Thinking hinders survival by introducing a delay to action. You become totally dependent on your subconscious and therefore a purely emotional response, or gut instinct. In fairness, in caveman days where the prefrontal cortex was nowhere near as well developed, there wasn't much to switch off! These days, where you could easily get all caught up in endless possibilities, your subconscious feels switching off the logical thoughts is necessary to survival, whether you agree or not. When faced with a very real threat like a sabre-toothed tiger, a split second can mean the difference between life and death. If you waste that time thinking, then you are likely to end up dead. You need to just act. So when faced with a threat that will hurt you or even kill you, you react without thinking. Your body is ready, and you rely exclusively on an instinctive response. This instinctive response is based on hundreds of years of survival training, so you're pretty good at it. Even now, if someone throws a punch at you then you will duck, flinch or throw your arms up. No one has to teach you to do this. It is innate.

You will notice most animals have these instincts. Hedgehogs roll into a ball. Chameleons freeze and blend into their surroundings. A herd of gazelles will run and rely on their speed to get them clear of the threat. Animals either learn the right way to react to protect themselves, or they die trying. If they don't adapt then evolution will mean they don't stay around for very long.

What I find interesting is how you are able to develop those instinctive reactions in situations where there is no caveman precedent for them. The introduction of flight simulators into pilot training made a massive difference to flight safety. It is not instinctive to know what to do when an engine fails and you need to land. It is not a situation your subconscious has ever had to deal with, so switching off the ability to think straight could have lethal consequences. Using a flight simulator, a pilot can go through the same scenario again and again until they are able to instinctively make the right choices even when they can no longer think straight.

Anyway, back to the sabre-toothed tiger. So here you are in the caveman days all geared up for having the best chance possible to stay alive. You can react instantly to a threat, and your mind and body are in harmony enough that your reactions increase your odds of survival. All good. You might have already worked out the problem here though. There are no sabre-toothed tigers any more, and in fact there are no predators for humans that threaten our daily existence.

If Something Upsets You, You Are Going to Die!

What I want you to do now is re-visit the paragraph about the physical reaction that is triggered when you are under threat:

> *A physical change happens. Your heart rate increases as blood begins to pump around your body faster. Your breath gets shorter. You are now in a heightened state of alert. Your body is ready to react.*

Sound familiar? Can you think of any situation where you have experienced this? What label did you give it: panic, anxiety, nerves, excitement? The thing is, while that response makes total sense when being attacked by a sabre-toothed tiger, it doesn't make quite as much sense when you have to stand up in front of an audience and deliver a presentation. Yet somehow, exactly the same response is triggered as if you are facing a sabre-toothed tiger.

If you have ever experienced anxiety or even a full-blown panic attack, I want you to think back to that time for a moment. If you replaced the thing that triggered the anxiety with a sabre-toothed tiger, would your reaction make more sense?

Lisa's Story – A Fear of Speaking to Groups

Lisa was a confident and outgoing person. If you put her in a room full of people, she had no problems finding someone to talk to. In her job, she regularly coordinated events and activities. When she talked about her work and being around people, her face lit up.

The problem came when Lisa had to talk to a few people at one time. In a meeting, if the organiser went round asking people to introduce themselves to the group, Lisa would freeze. The normally bubbly and socially engaging lady found her heart would start racing and her mouth would dry up. It got so bad that she would actually have a quiet word with the meeting organiser before it started and ask them not to do that to her. The harder she tried, the more extreme the reaction became, so that eventually she began to avoid anything if there was a risk where she would be in the spotlight. That's when she came to see me.

Lisa was frustrated that she couldn't just "get over it". She didn't normally suffer from anxiety. Her reaction to this situation made her feel out of control and question things in the wider context, not just this situation.

If you think about Lisa's story, it may sound familiar. Many people would approach this situation by helping Lisa deal with the physical symptoms associated with her anxiety. That can be very effective, but it never really deals with the Thing – the Thing that triggers her subconscious to take her into the freeze response in the first place.

What would happen if you replaced "talking to a group of people" with "facing a sabre-toothed tiger"? Does her response make more sense? In that context, the more Lisa forced herself into that situation, the more the subconscious got concerned about the risk to her. The more she tried to talk herself into confronting her fear, the more her subconscious ramped up the physical freeze response. It got so bad that she was starting to have panic attacks at just the thought of talking to a group of people. This makes no sense when the trigger for the fear is talking to a group of people, but makes lots more sense if it was a sabre-toothed tiger. The more she tried to confront her fear, the more her subconscious was saying, "Oh my god, you are going to die if you do that! Don't be stupid! Listen to me. Please. You are going to die!" Meanwhile, she is there giving herself a hard time because, while she sees talking to a group as a trivial thing, her subconscious sees her engaging with a sabre-toothed tiger.

Just because there are no sabre-toothed tigers around these

days, and in fact no predators for the human race, does not mean that your brain doesn't work in exactly the same way as it did in the caveman days. Your subconscious is constantly looking for things that are going to hurt you and triggering a fight, flight, freeze response. Simply put, everything is a sabre-toothed tiger as far as the subconscious is concerned.

Everything is a Sabre-Toothed Tiger

So what is "everything"? How does the subconscious decide what to protect against versus what is okay? That's the tricky bit. What we do know, is if the subconscious perceives something as a threat to your safety or wellbeing, then it triggers the same reaction it did in the caveman days. It is a simple, instant, and physical protection response.

What we also know is that, these days, the subconscious seems unable to distinguish between a physical threat and an emotional threat. This means that the same fight, flight, freeze response is triggered whether something is going to cause you physical pain or emotional pain. Putting this into context, if you remember, I told you that the subconscious is basically a very primitive emotional part of your brain that works on instinct and feelings, not logic and rational thought. So how on earth can it be the best judge of whether something will cause you emotional pain? And why can't you just tell it that it's okay?

The easiest way for me to begin to explain this is to look at phobias. A phobia is a heightened state of fear and according to Wikipedia:

A phobia (from the Greek: Phóbos, meaning "fear" or "morbid fear") is, when used in the context of clinical psychology, a type of anxiety disorder, usually defined as a persistent fear of an object or situation in which the sufferer commits to great lengths in avoiding, typically disproportional to the actual danger posed, often being recognized as irrational.

It is generally easy for us to see that phobias aren't rational. Think about someone you know that has a phobia. This person can behave in a way that is totally unfamiliar to you, as he turns into a wibbling wreck, when faced with the subject of his phobia. After, when the fear has passed, he returns to being the person you know.

A friend once told me a story of how she had been trapped in a room for over three hours because a spider was over the doorway. If you are not scared of spiders this seems ridiculous. But if you are scared of them, then your subconscious will do anything it can to keep you safe. It's not rational. It's primitive. It believes if you go near it, you will die and triggers the fight, flight, freeze response. Because a strong emotional response disengages the thinking brain, once a fear response has been triggered, you lose the ability to think your way round a problem. While others look on, someone with a phobic reaction to something is caught up in an emotional maelstrom, losing all ability to think straight. It is a survival response, a protection response. Because of this, the more you ignore it, the worse it usually gets.

Jo's Story – Travel Phobia

Jo came to me because he was scared of going on boats. He had family in Ireland so often needed to travel over there, and because he had young children, the easiest option was to go on a boat.

Initially, while he was not a big fan of going on a boat, it wasn't too much of a problem. Then on one trip he encountered really bad weather, and it triggered a fear in him. From that point onwards he became more and more anxious before each trip. It got so bad that it began to affect other forms of transport that used to be okay, like planes and trains. The more he ignored it, the worse it got until he began avoiding taking trips.

Why Me?

So what makes one person react to something with anxiety, panic or even a full-on phobic response while someone else is totally okay with it? My mother is terrified of spiders. She will leave a room as quickly as she can when she spots one. Yet I am quite happy to let a spider run around on my hand. Maybe I'm just stubborn and like spiders because my mother is scared of them!

Certainly there is a precedent here for phobias and fears being passed down through the generations. The question is, do phobias get passed through nurture or genetically.

There is an experiment with monkeys, a ladder, bananas and cold water that lends credibility to the nurture argument. The experiment went as follows:

A group of scientists placed five monkeys in a cage and in the middle, a ladder with bananas on the top. Every time a monkey went up the ladder, the scientists soaked the rest of the monkeys with cold water. After a while, every time a monkey went up the ladder, the others beat up the one on the ladder. After some time, no monkey dared to go up the ladder regardless of the temptation. Scientists then decided to substitute one of the monkeys. The first thing this new monkey did was to go up the ladder. Immediately the other monkeys beat him up. After several beatings, the new member learned not to climb the ladder even though he never knew why. A second monkey was substituted and the same occurred. The first monkey joined in to beat up the second monkey. A third monkey was changed and the same was repeated. The fourth was substituted and the beating was repeated, and finally the fifth monkey was replaced. What was left was a group of five monkeys that, even though they had never received a cold shower, continued to beat up any monkey who attempted to climb the ladder. If it was possible to ask the monkeys why they would beat up all those who

attempted to go up the ladder ... I bet you the answer would
be ... "I don't know – that's how things are done around here."

In favour of the genetic argument, a calf will stay away from a
cattle grid even if it's never been near one before. In fact, lines
painted on a road are enough to stop a cow that has no experience
of a cattle grid. An experiment done on mice showed that the
babies of a mouse that was given electric shocks whenever it
smelt orange blossom also had the fear of the smell, even though
they had no idea why. Other mice didn't. So a phobia or fear can
certainly be passed down through the generations.

It can also be a new thing that is unique to you.

To some degree it almost doesn't matter where the phobia
came from when it comes to getting rid of it. You could take ten
people and ask them to talk about themselves in front of a group,
and only one of them might feel anxious. You can take a hundred
people and get them to travel on a boat, and again only one or
two of them might feel anxious. Whether it is inherited genetically or triggered by an event, fears are unique to you, your
subconscious and your rulebook. If you want to understand
where a fear or a phobia comes from, you need to rummage
around in the subconscious and dig out the rule that it is
following.

The thing that makes this even more complicated is the
situation where there isn't even an obvious physical threat. With
a spider, even though you know they can't hurt us, it makes sense
that you might be afraid of a creature that at some point could
have been harmful. It makes sense that you could be extremely
afraid of heights because there is a very real risk of harm if
something goes wrong. However, what about fear of speaking to
a group of people? What is the risk with that? In that situation,
the subconscious is using a rule based on something that hurt
you emotionally to trigger a protection response.

Closer Look: Lisa's Story

Let's look again at Lisa who had a rule in her rulebook that said, "If you talk to a group of people you will die."

The first thing I did in this case was a bit of pattern matching to understand when the fear was triggered and when it wasn't. This allowed me to get a better feel for the Thing that was underneath the fear.

I established that if she was in a room full of people she was fine, even if there were a few around her. I established that she was okay talking one to one about herself. I also established that standing on a stage or even at the front of the room was just as scary as sitting round a table talking. So I now knew it was triggered when the spotlight was on her.

Lisa had a rule related to an event where the focus being on her made her feel bad. Due to the way the subconscious works, it was now triggering a fight, flight, freeze reaction to prevent her going into any situation that might make her feel as bad as that first event.

Closer Look: Jo's Story

Let's look again at Jo, who had developed such a high degree of anxiety about going on boats that it had now spread to other means of transport to the degree he was avoiding trips on planes and trains.

Once more I started with pattern matching. I discovered that the phobia had been triggered by the event with the very bad weather. Before that, he could think of boat trips and smile at the fun he had. His anxiety had spread to planes and trains, but he could take short train trips with no problems. He was perfectly fine in a car either driving or as a passenger. He had no problems with fear of bad weather when he was in a car or at home. So it wasn't the weather that triggered the fear, it was a combination of the weather and being on a form of transport that was very susceptible to the weather.

It was clear that his rulebook had something in it about being on a form of transport that could be affected by weather and that meant he was at risk of death.

Getting Rid of the Trigger

Due to the limited capacity of the subconscious to understand the full multidimensional nuances of what is happening around you in childhood, miscalculations easily happen. Things go into the rulebook that shouldn't really be there to protect you from perceived danger.

If you want to get rid of a phobia, you need to stop the protection reaction happening, which means you need to find the rule in the rulebook that equates to: "If you do X then you will die." Once you have found it then it's as simple as just rubbing it out – correcting the miscalculation so the protection reaction is no longer triggered. This may sound like an oversimplification, but in practice this is exactly how it works. After all, the thing that makes one person afraid and another totally fine is just the existence of the rule in the rulebook. You are no longer in the caveman days so talking to a group of people (no matter how nervous it makes you!) is not going to result in death. If the subconscious was not programmed to protect you, and if protection did not equate to stopping you being eaten or hurt physically, then this would never be an issue.

Because the rule is in the subconscious (and remember this is 90% of the thoughts through the day), to change it you need to engage with that part of the brain. It is not necessary to use techniques to take you into a hypnotised state to do this. You just need to talk about the problem, and your mind will automatically take you into your problem state – a trance state. This is a trance state because it is your subconscious we are working with, not your rational and logical conscious thoughts.

The Solution: Lisa's Story

We know that somewhere in Lisa's rulebook was a rule that related to a risk with the focus being on her. My job was to find that rule and remove it.

To do this I got her to focus on the feeling, and then I asked her subconscious to travel back to the event first connected to being aware of that feeling. For Lisa it took her back to being ten years old and sitting an exam. This was the point at which a rule had gone into the rulebook about a fear of failure. At ten years old your ability to understand more adult concepts such as "it's just an exam and it won't matter in the bigger picture of your life" or "if you fail it doesn't mean anything about you" is not fully developed. As a result, a rule went into her rulebook that said, "Failure is risky. Failure means that you get hurt. Failure means that you might die. I need to protect you from failure."

Once Lisa became an adult her subconscious started mapping different things that she did onto the rule by asking, "Does this mean failure?" If it did, then a protection response was triggered. In her case, speaking to a group of people meant that she might say something she'd regret. Or she could say it in a way that made people question her capabilities. That would mean failure. That would hurt. That is a bad thing!

So we deleted the rule. We deleted it by allowing her to pass a lesson to the ten year old version of herself that showed her subconscious that failure wasn't a big deal. She showed her younger self that she had been very successful in life and that none of it had to do with exam results. She showed her how little exams at such a young age mattered to her future. Without the risk of failure being a problem, there was no need for a rule and it was gone.

From that point forward, Lisa was able to easily speak to groups of people without any sort of protective trigger firing off.

The Solution: Jo's Story

Jo had a rule in his rulebook that had something to do with being on a form of transport that could be affected by weather, a rule that meant he was at risk of death!

Now I needed to find that rule and change it.

To do this I got him to focus on the feeling, and then I asked his subconscious to travel back to the event first connected to being aware of that feeling. For Jo it took him back to when he was five years old and at the fair with his mother. He wanted to go on the Ferris wheel, but his mother told him that it was very dangerous. She was apparently scared of all the rides. It is natural for you to adopt fears from your parents. It makes very good sense if you look at it in caveman survival terms where you may not be sure about what is dangerous and what is safe. As a result of learning from his mother's fear, a rule had gone into his book to be scared of stuff that moved, that was high up, that was exposed... I don't know how exactly it was worded, but that didn't matter. I now knew what event had created a rule in the rulebook.

With Jo you might wonder why he hadn't always followed that rule. Why had he not always been scared of boats and planes? When he had been on the boat in the bad weather, his subconscious had accessed that particular page for the first time. Once the rule had been accessed it was impossible for his subconscious to forget it, so it kept on mapping more and more similar situations to that rule. Survival is not just an instinctive skill – it is also enhanced through learning.

We deleted the rule by allowing him to see that the fear of the Ferris wheel came from his mother. He was able to see that he was really excited about the fair and disappointed about not being allowed on the rides. It was his mother's fear and not his.

From that point forward he was able to travel on boats and

planes again. In fact he took a trip out on a boat just for the fun of getting out there.

We can see how the software and algorithms that govern our thought processes are out-dated. Evolution has not changed this. If our subconscious could recognise the fact that we are no longer under threat from predators, it could stand down from trying so hard to protect us. Most of the things we get anxious or phobic about simply would not exist. Of course, there is a still a need for a certain level of caution – for safety and protection. It is good to be afraid of heights – just not phobic. It is good to be scared of animals that can harm you like snakes – just not phobic. Feeling nervous before a performance can actually be used to give you focus and enhance your performance. It shouldn't make you sick, and it shouldn't prevent you choosing to perform in the first place.

It is time that the first caveman rule – react first or die trying – had a bit of an update!

Fooling the Child – Treating Fears as Real

When someone you know is scared of spiders, do you join in? When a spider enters the room, do you run and grab a spear and then fall back yelling, "Fear not, I shall protect you!"? Or do you stand there amused for a while and observe the person you know turn into an out-of-control wreck before trying to persuade them that a spider is harmless? Probably the latter, right?

We don't tend to take other people's fears seriously. This can also be true when your child tells you they are scared of something. The thing is, though, that the fear is in his head. So is the way you see things. Eyes don't see. The brain sees based on the image received by the eyes. This is why there are so many optical illusions out there – because it is pretty easy to fool the brain. To the person afraid of the spider, that fear is as real as if they have a sabre-toothed tiger in front of them. No amount of reasoning is going to get rid of that fear.

To deal with a fear you need to treat the fear as real, because to the subconscious, it is real.

Wouldn't it be great if you could bring up your children with the resilience to learn to overcome the things that they are scared of, without needing help from anyone else? It would be a useful skill to get them through many different things in later life. Dealing with a fear in the right way can stop it becoming a rule in the rulebook.

It goes against your natural instinct as a parent to allow your child to find her own solution when she is upset, and all you want to do is make it better for them. But in this situation your natural instinct, to tell them everything is okay, is not going to make it better at all. It isn't all right. Your child is scared of something, and to her subconscious that something may as well be a sabre-toothed tiger – it is that real. So the best way to deal with it is to treat it as real.

If there really is a monster under the bed, how would you deal with it? Now, more importantly, ask your child how she would deal with it because she has a much better imagination. Try saying something like, "It's in your head, so I can't see what it looks like; can you describe it to me?" and then, "What do you think is the best way to beat it?"

I often find it helps to explain what that means. I tell my daughter that what she watches on TV is made up in someone's head. It's not real, but it's someone's clever ideas from their head. Whatever she is scared of is the same. It's in her head, but I can't see it, so I need her to tell me. Then I ask her how she can beat it. It may not be obvious, so I will suggest things like wearing a cape, or a magic wand. When she was scared of zombies (too much Scooby Doo!), she pulled out a flamethrower in her head and zapped them. When she was scared of a monster in the middle of the night, she decided to burp in its mouth!

The key thing to remember is that by teaching your child they have all the resources in their head to deal with their fears, they should find that as they reach adulthood, they naturally just deal with stuff, instead of expecting anyone else to help them.

Caveman Rule Number 2 –
If Your Parents Don't Love You, You'll Die!

If you are a cavebaby it is critical that you have a good bond with your cavemum. If you don't, then she is not going to feed you. It was tough in the caveman days. Nobody would step in and look after you. If your mother didn't feed you, then you'd die. As you grew up it was critical to keep the bond strong. If this bond is broken you are going to die.

This means as a cavebaby you need to be pretty savvy. You need to go beyond the cute smiles and giggles. You need to watch your mum closely. You need to copy what she does. You need to stay away from what makes her cross and do more of what makes her happy. Beyond that you need to adopt her beliefs and values to keep the bond strong because you want her to keep feeding you.

Have you wondered why, when babies are born, they look most like their dads? The mother has carried them for nine months and has an innate bond. The father has nothing. So in those precious few days when a baby is first born, they look more like their father than their mother. It's all about what gives you the best chance of surviving.

However, you may have noticed that The Caveman Rules of Survival no longer apply to the modern day. In the main children aren't allowed to die because of a lack of bond with their mother. But the weird thing is that you are still programmed to behave as if you were. You have an inherent behaviour to connect everything that happens in your childhood to a meaning. That meaning is pretty simple:

Does this event that just happened mean they love me more or less?

If it is more, then you do more of it. If it is less, you do less of it. Either way you are likely to end up with a rule in your rulebook connecting the event to how much it made you feel loved. Let me give you an example.

> *You are eight years old and sat at the kitchen table at home doing your homework. You've been stuck on a particular question for a long time. Your dad walks in from a day at work, and you say, "Dad, can you help me with my homework; I'm really stuck on this question?"*
>
> *"For goodness sake!" snaps your dad, "I've only just walked through the door, and I haven't even taken my coat off yet. Why can't you just get on and sort it yourself for once?"*

And with that he heads off to his study to regroup. Later on, he doesn't remember a thing about what happened.

Now according to The Caveman Rules of Survival, if your parents don't love you, then you will die, so let's look at how this might be connected. You asked for help, and your dad shouted at you. Your dad shouting at you is not a good thing because it means he doesn't love you. Your dad not loving you means you are going to die. So if asking for help leads to your dad not loving you, then the lesson would be: "Don't ask for help because you will die." A rule goes into your rulebook. In your adult life you find that you are not one of these people that asks for help when you need it because it just makes you feel really uncomfortable. You have no idea why; all you know is that you don't do it, and the more you think about doing it, the worse the feeling gets.

The thing is that you could put hundreds of children in that situation and only one of them may end up with a rule in their rulebook. The others would just pass it off as an insignificant event. I don't think the decision on whether to put it in the rulebook has anything to do with the sensitivity of the child. It probably has more to do with the significance of the incident in the context of all other incidents in life up to that point. It may be that something had gone before that was similar and had an even clearer connection, so that a rule was already in the rulebook and another would be redundant.

It does not just happen with bad stuff either. Let me give you another example:

At six years old you are coming back from the shop with your mother. Because you are six you are running everywhere as usual. You trip up and scrape your knee. As you stand in front of your mother in tears, she pulls out a lollipop and gives it to you to suck on.

Remember, the rule here is that if your parents don't love you, then you will die. You fell and you hurt yourself. Your mother gave you a sweet to make you feel better when you were hurting. The logical conclusion is that your mother must love you when she gives you a sweet to stop you feeling hurt. So a rule goes into your rulebook that says: "Sweets make you feel loved." As an adult when you are upset in any way and you need to feel comforted and loved, you turn to sweet things to help you cope. You have tried for many years to give up sweet things, and when everything is going okay you manage fine, but when you are stressed or upset it's the first thing you turn to.

So all through your childhood you are making connections between things that happen and what they mean in terms of love. Your subconscious believes that this is critical to survival, even though it no longer is.

Let's look at a couple of case studies to see how easy it is for these connections be made.

Bill's Story – If He Carried on Eating This Way He Would End Up Overweight

Bill was worried about gaining weight. Most of the time he was okay, but whenever things got stressful for him he turned to food. His food of choice was anything sweet. Cakes were the things he found hardest to resist. He wasn't overweight by much but could tell from his behaviour around food that if he didn't change, he would end up with a problem.

Jane's Story – She'd Tried Every Diet and Was Desperate to Lose the Weight

Jane had struggled with her weight her whole life. She had done pretty much every diet going and, while she had lost weight on countless occasions, she had always put it back on ... and then some! She came to me as a last resort because she'd tried everything else and felt, because of her terrible willpower, she needed help with her head.

The thing about this caveman rule is that it's probably the most emotionally loaded of them all. The belief that you are not lovable can lead to such a strong subconscious need for protection that the feelings can become too much to bear. It is very primal. If you are not lovable, then you will not be cared for. If you are not cared for, you will die. When these emotions are brought about by events when you are a child, you often don't have the capacity to cope with them. You certainly don't have the capacity to understand them fully or the reasons for the behaviours of the adults in those events.

The consequences can be wide-ranging and affect you well into your adult life. In fact, many people never get over the belief that they are unlovable. When the pain of emotions becomes unbearable, then you need to do something to stop it. Some people turn to an emotional crutch – something that dampens down the intensity of the emotions. This can be alcohol, drugs, gambling or even food. It doesn't really matter what the substance is, the important thing is to bury those painful emotions that have such severe consequences as far as your subconscious is concerned. Addictions can provide a convenient solution. Worst case scenario is that you spend your emotional energy on the consequences of the addiction (guilt, self-loathing, physical withdrawal) instead of the thing that originally triggered you to turn to them. Self-harm can also provide a way out. It's a lot easier to deal with a physical pain. You can stick a band aid on it. You can watch it stop bleeding, and you can make it bleed again. It's a controllable pain. Bingeing and purging are also a form of self-harm. If it gets too bad it can lead to attempted, or even successful, suicide.

Feeling that you are not loved can have significant consequences for the rest of your life.

The Connection Between Caveman Rule Number 2 and Weight

Weight is a fascinating area when you approach it from a psychological point of view. It may not surprise you by now to hear that there is a caveman connection made in your head when you go on a diet. Whether it is depriving yourself of food in quantity, or even depriving yourself of significant food groups, your mind makes a connection between diet and survival. "I know this!" it says. "This is famine!" It then enters a mode where it does everything it can to survive this period of famine. It has no idea how long it's going to last, but what it does know from caveman experience, is that periods of famine are fairly normal.

Think of how it worked in the caveman days. One day you would get lucky, and you and your tribe would capture a woolly mammoth. This would last you a good few weeks. After that, it may have been weeks or more before you were able to get another catch suitable for feeding the whole tribe. Your body needed to be able to adapt to the cycle of feast and famine, in such a way as you had the best chance of surviving. What this meant in practice is that during a period of famine, your body would shut down all unnecessary functions. The focus would be on conserving your current reserves because you didn't know how long you would need them. You needed to get as much energy and nutrition as you could from what you ate so that you weren't eating into your fat reserves too soon. Then, at some point, the famine would be over. What your mind and body knew, however, is that there would be another period of famine along soon. When the famine was over, it would be critical to stock up again as quickly as you possibly could. Instead of taking the nutrition from the food, you wanted to stockpile as much in your body as you could, in preparation for the next period of famine.

Because of The Caveman Rules of Survival, when you go on a modern day diet your mind interprets this as a period of famine. Metabolism is slowed down and the focus becomes about getting everything you can from whatever you put into your body. The nature of a diet is that you will always have "time off"; a birthday party, a holiday, or another special event where you don't want to limit what you eat. Your body then interprets that as a time of feast and does everything it can to stock up again. Whatever the reason for this break in your diet, it doesn't matter to your brain. As far as it's concerned, it knows what is going on, and it engages The Caveman Rules. This is why diets don't work as a long term solution. It is not about willpower. It is about a failure to understand the workings of the mind-body connection.

Why do we feel diets are necessary? What is it that makes it so difficult to eat the right food to give us just enough energy? The primitive animal part of our brain says, "If there is food there, eat it." but we are not animals. We have the prefrontal cortex. So what makes us lose control of our eating habits despite having willpower and self-control?

This is when we come back to the three caveman rules of survival.

Generally, when you find that you have a battle going on in your head, a battle between your conscious freewill and a subconscious voice, then there is a caveman rule somewhere behind it.

When I work with weight loss clients I look for two things:

1. I look for anything to do with the way you see yourself. Weight can be a protection from being hurt. It may be that being fat makes you feel like you won't be judged for your personality. It is a lot easier to believe that someone doesn't like you for the way you look (something you can technically change) than for who you are. It may also be that it is protecting you physically. It may be that being fat stops you being shapely, and so, at a subconscious level, you can believe you are not attractive. This can be summed up as self-esteem and often relates to the way you think other people see you. Eating is basically a side effect of the need to keep the weight on for protection. Often this relates to Caveman Rule Number 3 – if you're not part of a pack you will die.

2. I am looking for the emotional meaning that food has for you. Is there a particular type of food that you find hardest to resist, or is it a quantity based thing? Is there a particular time of day when you find it impossible to apply willpower to not eating? Addictions are about either dampening a strong emotion with a substance or replacing/satisfying an emotional need with a substance. Unlike most addictions, food is an addiction you can't get over by abstaining. We all need to eat to live. This means no matter how hard you work to resist the emotional drive to eat, at some point you will still need to eat. That really sucks and can make it one of the most difficult addictions to get over.

Many of us have fond memories associated with food. Maybe it's a special meal you had or even the smell of a certain food like popcorn that takes you back to a childhood memory. Almost every memory I have from my childhood has food associated with it because I was deprived of food as a young child. Like many of my clients, there are certain foods that make me smile when I think of them. Food can be like music. It brings forward either fond or not so good memories. This is normal behaviour. The problem comes when you have an emotional attachment to food that has been equated to survival and therefore has resulted in a rule. When food is about survival, you can find yourself stuck with behaviours you can't overcome no matter how hard you try.

I often see clients who have an eating disorder, such as bulimia or binge eating. If they end up interacting with the medical profession, they are treated like they are making a choice. They are given nutritional advice, suggestions for pattern interruptions that will allow them to control their behaviour, and through self-help groups, they can learn a lot about different ways to live with their problem. The problem is that group therapy can have a similar downside to being in prison; it can be a great way of getting new ideas on how to do something from a group of people with similar experiences! When I was younger, there were a lot of things going on in my life that were causing me significant emotional distress. At that time there was very little out there about self-harm. I know that if I had come across something that described how you can self-harm, I would have tried it out myself. When you are already looking for solutions, people with a common experience can be a great source of ideas – even if those ideas are potentially bad ones!

It is my belief that, because of the way the brain works, this is not about choice. With an eating disorder, food is an addiction and should be treated in the same way as you would treat an addiction to any other substance. Find the thing that is driving the need for the addiction and change that. Because food is a substance that we can't abstain from, it is rarely treated as an addiction. Unless you get rid of the emotional connection that drove the need to turn to the substance, then you will potentially always be locked in a battle with yourself. Even if you are winning for a while, at some point you will be exhausted, or something will draw your resources away from the battle, and the addiction will take hold again. This is why you hear these sad stories about celebrities who have had an addiction that they have been clear of for years and then something happens, and they end up dead of an overdose.

Closer Look: Bill's Story

Let's look again at Bill, who had such a strong attachment to cakes that he couldn't resist them.

When I was looking at patterns with Bill, I found that he didn't really seem to have any issue with the way people saw him. The reason for not gaining any more weight was primarily for health reasons. When I was talking to him about his behaviour around food, I found that eating cake made him feel good. The word comfort came up. It can be tricky to get the emotion that eating food gives a client because there is often such a strong conscious sense of guilt and responsibility. They feel a failure for not being able to resist. They don't realise it's just their subconscious protecting them. As a result, when I first ask them what positive thing they get from food, they shrug and say something like: "Nothing. It's stupid."

There is a little trick that I use when I am struggling to find out what the positive intention is behind a certain behaviour or belief. You can try it yourself and see what you discover. This is a word association game, so it's really important to pay attention to the very first word that pops into your head. Remember how I said that the subconscious reacts instantly? Well, we need to make use of that to make this exercise work well.

1. Write down a statement that describes the behaviour you are struggling with at the top of a piece of paper. For Bill it would be "eating cakes".

2. Underneath, write "BAD" on the left and "GOOD" on the right and draw a line down the middle to separate them.

3. Name something bad about X. For Bill it would be: "Name something bad about eating cakes". It's important to ask for something bad first because that's a lot easier to think of.

4. Then we want a word for the GOOD column so ask: "Name something good about X". For Bill it would be: "Name something good about eating cakes".

5. Swap back and forth between the good and bad question until no more words come to mind. Remember to trust the first word that comes to mind and to avoid over-analysing your answers.

When you have finished, look back at the words you have written. Anything in the bad column usually relates to a conscious evaluation. It often reflects longer term consequences of your problem. Anything in the good column usually relates to what your subconscious thinks you are getting from the behaviour. This is the biggest clue to what the protection intent behind the behaviour is. For Bill, in his bad column, he had "health, weight and out-of-control". In his good column he had "happy" and "comfort".

Closer Look: Jane's Story

Let's look at Jane again who had tried every diet going and was desperate to lose weight. She believed she had terrible willpower because she couldn't stick to a diet. She always put the weight back on. It was a relief for her to know that it was normal behaviour, and it really wasn't her fault. She felt everyone was looking at her and thinking how fat she was. She couldn't stand to look at herself in the mirror. The problem was, the worse she felt about her failure to lose weight, the more she sought comfort from food, and the cycle was getting worse. Jane was binge eating on a regular basis which triggered a deep self-loathing both for the weight it put on and the perceived lack of control she had over food and herself.

There were clearly issues to do with self-esteem as well as an emotional connection to food. This is often the case with clients. I usually find it takes some work to get through the layers, starting with the emotional behaviour around food, and then once you have sorted that, beginning to work on the issue with the way they see themselves.

You can see from my example with the scraped knee how easy it is to connect food to emotion. Think about it: how many times have you used or been given food as a treat or a reward for good behaviour? I had one client who used to go to a cafe with his mother after every dentist trip for cake. It took the worry out of the dentist trip by having something nice at the end of it. Can you imagine what that client did whenever he was worried about anything? Eat, of course. If it had been a comic or magazine they got instead, then that would have been a far less damaging emotional connection. How many of you were made to finish everything on your plate by your parents because it was wasteful not to? Maybe they went as far as to say there were children starving in Africa. We are surprised that generations of children grew up to be adults with problems with portion control, when we have been brought up to finish everything on the plate and have learnt to ignore the full signals that our body naturally sends.

When I was a young child I slipped and gouged my face on a nail. My mother gave me a hard candy to stop me crying, not realising that crunching when you have blood pouring out of a gash in your face is not the best idea! I now have a soft spot for that same candy that makes me feel comforted when I eat them.

It seems to be natural for us to use food to make situations more tolerable for children. It's no surprise really that we end up growing up with food meaning so much more than fuel.

The thing is, children know how to listen to their bodies. If they aren't hungry, they won't eat. If they are hungry, they will eat until they are full and then stop when they've had enough. It is adults that impose a different set of rules on them – rules about when they should eat, how much they should eat and what sort of food is okay. Adults can stop the natural process of listening to the body in favour of some ideal about what is right and wrong. Once you have stopped listening to your body, it's pretty hard to re-establish that mind-body connection.

If you think you have a problem with ignoring the messages your stomach sends you, you can re-boot the mind/body connection by eating mindfully. Don't do anything else while eating. Don't use your phone or computer, watch TV or even read a book. Close your eyes. Notice the taste and texture of the food on your tongue. Notice, as you swallow each mouthful, how it feels when it hits your stomach. Eating mindfully can be the first step in reconnecting your mind and body; allowing them to communicate in real time about what you are eating.

Getting Rid of the Trigger

The nice thing about a caveman rule that connects events to love is that it is almost always blatantly obvious that it's not valid when you go back and look at the actual event that created the connection. This is because, invariably, the rule was established when you were at an age where your view of the world was very literal. As an adult, you don't have the cardboard box on your head and can fully see what is going on. Hindsight provides great insight.

Let me give you an example which has always stuck with me for its simplicity. I had a client who was struggling to lose weight. She found she had to eat the food that was there. When we went on a Thing hunt, I discovered that the thing she got from eating was comfort. We then went looking for a rule where the emotional connection was made. Her subconscious showed us an event where she was about two years old. She was in the kitchen in her high chair, and there was a recently finished, bowl of baked beans in front of her. She was aware of feeling very lonely in the kitchen. Then her mother walked in and, when she saw that she had eaten all of her beans, gave her a hug and told her what a good girl she was.

See the connection? It's pretty obvious really isn't it? "I ate all my beans which means my mum loves me. If I want to make sure my mum loves me, I must make sure I eat all my food." It really is that easy for a connection to be made. All we had to do was break the connection between the food in that moment and the feeling of being loved. As a two-year-old it was hard to see. As an adult, my client could easily reflect back on all the things about that moment, and many others in her life, which showed her that her mother loving her had nothing to do with food. She passed that lesson to the two-year-old version of herself, and the emotional connection was broken. Incidentally, she always used to hate baked beans, and that changed too!

Anyway let's look again at the two clients and how that same approach was used to free them up of their behaviour around food.

The Solution: Bill's Story

Once I knew that Bill found eating cakes comforting, I had the Thing that his subconscious was using to make it impossible to resist the cakes. Now it was just a matter of finding the point at which the connection was made between comfort from eating food and protection. I needed to find the point at which a rule went into his rulebook.

When Bill was a young child he used to go to his gran's house to play. Like many grans, his used to bake lots of lovely cakes. At home things were difficult with his parents, so his time at his gran's house was filled with wonderful happy memories. Because as you grow up you see the world through a limited view, he associated the love he got from his gran with the cakes she baked him. As an adult, when he was stressed or needed to feel loved, it made total sense that he turned to cakes. At the simplest level the rule in his rulebook said: "Because your gran made you cakes, it means she loves you, and because she loves you, then you will get fed, and therefore you won't die." In that context, he would be crazy not to eat the cakes when to resist would ultimately mean death!

To change this, all I had to do was guide him to view that moment with adult eyes. I guided him to see, with his adult perspective, how there was so much more to spending time with his gran than the food he ate while he was there. He was able to notice stuff he'd never noticed that his gran did with him. He was able to remember that being at his gran's house was so much happier because of how difficult things were at home, and it was nothing to do with the cakes.

Changing this removed any emotional connection to the cakes. Then he was free to choose to eat them or not eat them in a way he never had been before. Bill rarely eats cakes these days. They just don't do anything for him. He can happily walk past a cake shop with barely a glance.

The Solution: Jane's Story

With Jane, once I had established that food was more than fuel, it was a matter of tracking down which situations drove her to use food as an emotional crutch. Were there specific emotions or events that made her turn to food? What was it that triggered a binge? Most people binge in secret and plan it. They will have food in the house that they can binge on when they need it. In the same way as an alcoholic will consume alcohol to drown out the feelings or give them the illusion of confidence, a binge eater will usually start on a binge to escape from some sort of intense emotion that they can't face dealing with.

As with anything, this was about finding the Thing. In this case I wanted to understand the first moment where the subconscious had made a connection between emotions and eating. I guessed it was going to be a negative emotion because when it is for a good feeling, like in Bill's story, it tends not to lead to a binge eating cycle.

We went back to a time when Jane was just a toddler. In the particular moment we went to, she was being given chocolate because she was crying. The chocolate was being shoved into her mouth by her mother to stop the crying. As she looked back, Jane remembered that it's what always happened. She had learnt at a young age that crying would be ignored, and if she kept on crying, then eventually all that would happen was that her mother would stick food in her mouth to shut her up. Looking back, it was obvious what the rule was: "When something makes you feel emotional, eating food will stop you having to feel those emotions." Basically, food replaced emotion for her from a very young age.

It was relatively simple to break that connection. As an adult it is easy to see that it is wrong for a mother to use food to shut up a child instead of attending to his or her emotional needs. To show this to her younger self, Jane took the chocolate away and gave herself a hug instead. The emotional connection to food was broken, and the binge eating stopped.

It is so easy for these miscalculations to happen – connections between events and love made entirely in error. If the subconscious could recognise the fact that in modern society there is little risk to being abandoned, then most of these rules would become obsolete. There is obvious evidence that we have already adapted to some degree. For example, that a rule can be written based on love of a range of significant adults, not just the mother, reflects this. If we were still on pure caveman rules, then the father would have no role in building these rules. In my experience, a rule that connects events and love can come from any significant adult – parents, grandparents, uncles and aunties, and even teachers (although that is less common). The only area they tend not to come from is siblings. I assume this is because siblings are also still learning to survive. That is not to say they can't, it's just that I have no evidence of it to date.

Fooling the Child – I Love You Even If...

When I first realised that the subconscious is connecting every-thing to love as we grow up, my daughter was four years old. It worried me. A lot. Like many other parents, I told her I loved her often. Clearly this was not enough to stop things going into the rulebook. It seems that no matter what I did, my daughter would grow up with a whole bunch of rules in her rulebook based on miscalculated connections to love.

It got me thinking: I wonder if there is really something I can do to change this? So I set about doing everything I could to break the connection between anything that happened in her life and what it meant to love. I came up with, "I love you even if..."

It's very simple really. If events can be interpreted by the subconscious as meaning something to love, then all I had to do was disassociate everything from love. The basic premise is: "No matter what you do, it won't affect how much I love you." I started off with the bigger stuff:

I love you even if I shout at you
I love you even if you shout at me
I love you even if you tell me you hate me
I love you even if I tell you off

Then I realised, if I really wanted to be sure that nothing was connected to love, then I needed to include everything, no matter how big or small. So I expanded it to the trivial stuff:

I love you even if you have a messy face
I love you even if you don't like tomatoes
I love you even if you burp

Now, there can be no doubt in my daughter's mind that things she does have no impact on how much I love her. She can be secure in that knowledge. She seems very balanced and secure in the love I have for her and very free in sharing how much she loves other people. What I won't know for another 10-15 years is whether her subconscious was taking it the same way!

Caveman Rule Number 3 –
If You Are Not Part of a Pack, You Will Die

It started like any other day. You got on your tiger skin, grabbed a spear and headed out with the gang to hunt. You knew you'd probably be gone a couple of days because the beasties you hunt tend to wander in packs. It's a good job the cavewomen will remain behind to keep the camp going. You try to travel light because you will need to be both fast and stealthy when it comes to the hunt. You and your fellow cavemen each carry your own weapon and a small portion of dried meats and berries wrapped in a leaf. You will find water along the way, and you won't be lighting any fires because you won't risk scaring off the prey. You know it will be a hard few days. You will cover many miles and will have to take your turn of watching the other guys through the night. But it will be worth it. If you are able to catch a big enough beastie, then you will have enough to feed the whole camp for a couple of weeks.

After two days of hiking you spot a herd of woolly mammoths. It's a reasonably large herd, which means there is a good chance of it having some younger and older ones. Easy pickings. There are ten of you. Any more and you wouldn't be able to travel fast enough. Too few and you would have no chance in the hunt. You have a plan. It's the one you always follow when hunting. You know it works. You take up position on the far side of the plain. Your job is to turn back the mammoth that the hunters have singled out if it looks like it will escape. It's the job you hate most because it's boring. Besides, if you see a woolly mammoth charging at you, then you aren't really going to be in a position to stop it on your own!

You set off first because you have the longest distance to cover. You have to be careful because, if the herd gets alerted to your presence, they will run before anyone gets a chance to single out the prey of choice. Unfortunately, on this day, you mess up and don't pay enough attention to the wind direction. As you near the end of the plain, nearly an hour later, the herd spooks and runs at full pelt. They may not look it, but those woolly mammoths can be fast when they get going. You're knocked over by one of them at the front and, although lucky enough to get knocked out of the way, you also spend a few hours unconscious.

When you come round there is no sign of the herd of woolly mammoths – or your fellow hunters. You are all alone. This is not good. You are not the tracker so have no idea how to get back to camp. You barely have enough food for the next two days, and you have no means of making a fire, so you are exposed to the predators through the night.

The prognosis is not good. As a caveman it was almost impossible to survive without your pack.

What has this got to do with the modern day? You don't need to be part of a pack to survive these days. You are perfectly capable of surviving without any other human contact. In fact, social contact is more a nice-to-have for your mental health and wellbeing than it is a matter of survival. However, what you know already is that your subconscious is still working on The Caveman Rules of Survival.

So how does this caveman rule get translated these days? Consider the following scenario:

You are thirteen years old, and it is break time at high school. You got your hair cut yesterday, and you are not that happy with the style, but you know it always takes you a couple of days to get used to it. As you wander around chatting to your friends, one of the girls in the popular group looks at you and then turns to her friends laughing. You are sure it's about you and your haircut. You get that sinking feeling inside. You are different. Someone is laughing at you. Then in jumps your subconscious with a whole bunch of connections. If she is laughing at you, then you don't fit in; if you don't fit in, then you are not part of the pack. Oh my god, if you are not part of the pack you are going to die!

This is why the scale of your reaction to feeling singled out, or not fitting in, is way out of line with what is actually happening. Any evidence of something where you don't fit in is taken as a sign by your subconscious that you are in danger of not having a pack. It doesn't matter if it's a casual comment with no thought behind it or deliberate bullying, the subconscious will still take it as significant, and a rule will go in your rulebook.

This same pack mentality also drives other elements of your behaviour. Have you ever heard the phrase "a chain is only as strong as its weakest link"? When you are working in a team, where your very survival is dependent on the strength of each person, this is a very pertinent phrase. There is no room in the team for someone who is too weak to pull his own weight. This means that when you are in a pack or any sort of group, then you will naturally identify and move away from what is perceived as the weakest person. This is not a conscious choice. It is not being mean or unfriendly. It is a natural survival instinct. At the same time, you will naturally gravitate to the person you perceive as the strongest in the pack. Success in a hunt was significantly improved by having a strong leader. People often talk about how weird it is that women are attracted to the bad guys but want a relationship with the good guys.

Attraction is primal, but settling down in the modern day is not about the ability of the male to go out and hunt. The same happens at school. You might hate the popular kids, and they might be totally different to you in terms of their interests, etc. but at the end of the day there is still a part of you that wants them to like you and wants to impress them.

This is a rule where the older you get, the more significant this rule seems to become. In fact I don't believe this rule begins to even enter into your rulebook until you are approaching puberty.

As a young child you are your world. You are not too concerned about the role you play in the world, or the group, or about the way you compare with the other children. Children younger than five generally don't play well with other children. Even when they are older, and have learnt to play with others, while they are still prepubescent, there is less significance to not fitting in.

When my daughter was five years old she started school. She had already been at pre-school for a couple of years, but full time school is a bit of a step up. It was a small school, so she was in a class that was made up of children from the ages of five through eight. It was interesting, and very challenging, watching the social dynamics of this relatively young group of children. When she was in pre-school she didn't seem to have any awareness of whether any of the other children liked her or not. What we discovered when she started school was that her interpretation of how good a day she had was dependent on who she'd been sat next to and who played with her during breaktime.

One day when I picked her up from school she had a face like thunder. When I asked her what was wrong she said, "I've had a horrible day!" This is every parent's nightmare. Anything that might mean that your child doesn't like going to school is something that can make life very difficult. But I was aware she was only five, so there were a limited number of things that could really cause a problem. "Oh dear," I replied. "What happened?" She looked at me with a frown and said, "Everyone was being mean to me!" This is pretty typical of the limited understanding of a child of her age. Things are very black and white, so when she talks about the opinions of others, it is always "everybody" or "nobody". She simply didn't comprehend that different people had different opinions. You can see that if a rule goes into the rulebook at this age it is likely to be a blatant miscalculation because of this limited understanding.

Anyway, I needed to move on from her definition of

"everyone was being mean" and understand where it had come from. I was pretty sure it wasn't everyone and also pretty sure that they weren't really being mean, or certainly not intentionally anyway! I replied with, "Everyone?" and when she insisted it was everyone, I asked if the headmistress was being mean to her. "No." And if the teacher of the other class was being mean. "No, all the kids," she said. To which I responded, "All of the kids? Even the ones in the other class?" "No, just the ones on my table." This was enough to destroy the myth that "everyone" was being mean to her. In their attempt to make sense of things, it is very easy for younger children to classify stuff into broad categories. They haven't had the range of experiences that will teach them what an exception is and what is normal. This can lead to this tendency to treat individual things or events as normal.

She went on to tell me the story of how she had been sat at the table with the other kids. As I mentioned, it's a mixed class, so the children were aged 5-8. They were colouring in. Apparently some of the children were "telling her off" because she was supposed to use certain pens. The teacher came over and told the other children, "Stop being mean and let her use the pens she wants." Bingo. While the teacher meant well, what she had actually done was defined that particular interaction as kids being mean to my daughter. When she told me she'd had a horrible day because "everyone" was mean to her, it all came from that simple sentence used by the teacher, who was actually trying to be nice.

"Everyone is being mean to me" is a statement that implies there is something wrong with the behaviour of everyone else. She was aware that she didn't like what the other children were doing when they told her off for using the wrong pens. She then was given a label for that behaviour by her teacher when she said they were being "mean", and so it became a bad day because some children demonstrated behaviour that she didn't like.

At no point did this turn into "and that means I am..." or "because they did this I am..." statement. While a kid is prepubescent, the significance is an external one. It might make them miserable, and it might make them want to avoid school, but that's because of stuff that is happening in their environment. Take them out of the environment and everything becomes okay again.

In this instance I helped my daughter put the teacher's comment in a different context, based on my experience and understanding of how the subconscious works. "Wasn't it nice of the teacher to help the other kids understand that it was okay for you to use the pens?" You only ever know your own thoughts, so sometimes it can feel like everything in the world is about you. Helping my daughter understand, even in the smallest way, that the stuff that happens is rarely about her allows her to learn the resilience which she will need in later life.

I am not saying that feeling singled out or picked on doesn't hurt during your younger years. It very much does. I am also not saying that you won't remember those incidents and how they made you feel well into your adult life. I think you will. But something hurting you and being significant enough to remember is not the same as something that triggers a caveman-based need for protection in your subconscious. It is possible for something to hurt you without being life threatening. Your caveman brain is only interested in documenting the stuff that it regards as a threat to your survival into the rulebook.

If the situation I described with my daughter had happened when she was eleven, then she may have reached a different conclusion. Instead of remaining environmental, she might have begun to make it about her. She might have internalised it. Instead of it being about the other children being mean to her, she might have decided that there was something wrong with her. As your world expands you begin to become aware of the relationship between you and the people around you. Your decisions and choices are no longer made based on what pleases you alone, but now are influenced by the impact they have on other people. In my experience this starts to happen from the age of ten upwards – but I am no Piaget, so this is purely based on experience from working with my clients. At this point there are so many more opportunities to get things wrong because your subconscious believes they mean so much more than they do. For example:

The other girls don't have big hips like me which means I am different and there is something wrong with me.

I don't like football and my dad and brothers do, so there is something wrong with me.

I failed the test, so I must be stupid.

My sister is prettier than me and gets all the attention, so I must be ugly and unattractive.

I believe the rule of needing to be part of the pack really kicks in when you hit puberty. When you add in the "complication" of procreation into the things that the subconscious is responsible for, then your status as a male or a female becomes significant. Your status in the pack is no longer just about your skills and personality but expands to include your ability to help the whole race survive and grow stronger. That's a lot of pressure when you are a teenager and your hormones are all over the place! This is why the stuff that ends up as rules at this age so often translate into issues of self-esteem and self-worth as an adult.

Why is puberty significant? To understand this you have to remember that your brain is operating on caveman rules of survival. In the caveman days you would be looked after as a child until you were old enough to look after yourself. As a girl, as soon as you reached puberty you would be given a mate, and your job was to breed and keep the clan alive. The better you were at breeding, the more successful you were at attracting a mate, and the higher your status in the clan would be. As a boy, things would also change for you when you reached puberty. You would now be able to join in the hunts. You would be able to compete for seniority in the clan and eventually even have your own clan. Your strength and skills in hunting, and keeping everyone alive, would define your status in the clan.

In the caveman days, status equalled survival. And it still does. Actually it doesn't, but remember that your brain is still working on The Caveman Rules. As far as your subconscious is concerned, it is important to do everything you can to be part of the pack and to ensure that your status in the pack is as secure as it can be. This means that once you hit puberty, those things that used to be just environmental factors now become about status, and as a result, can lead to rules in the rulebook.

Prejudice, like racism, sexism and judgements based on class, are all born out of the caveman rule about being part of the pack and fitting in. They are born out of a primal need to classify people in such a way as you can easily determine if they will strengthen or weaken the group. There have been extreme examples of this over the years. Probably the most famous example was Hitler and his beliefs in white supremacy. He was trying to strengthen the pack by removing what he perceived as the weaker race, the Jews, from the gene pool. I am not saying for one minute that it was down to a caveman rule in his rulebook, but the foundation to his psychotic belief came from the caveman rule about being part of a pack. It is worth noting at this point that sometimes people just have defective wiring in their brain. This can lead to a lack of a moral compass or at least a very different one to everyone else. As a result, a person can become very dangerous, because, although still driven by The Caveman Rules, they also have the use of their prefrontal cortex to put crazy ideas into action.

However, moving on from the exceptions, let's return to the majority of the human race. Most of us have a pretty good moral compass that regulates our actions and the way we treat other people. In fact, in much of the time, instead of choosing to single someone else out for a perceived flaw, you are more likely to take it on yourself as a fault, because at the end of the day you can only control your own survival. If there is a perception that something is wrong, then you take it upon yourself to correct it. We call this self-esteem, and it's very easy to end up with low self-esteem but a bit trickier to build it back up again. This rule of needing to be part of the pack drives you to compare yourself to others at all sorts of levels. It is fundamental to fitting in, as far as your subconscious is concerned, to understand your place in any group of people and behave accordingly. The understanding of how you do this in the most effective way possible is established in your rulebook during childhood.

As with the other two rules, all through childhood your subconscious is looking for things that will lead you to fit in more and for things that will hurt you because you don't fit in as much. Early on these are just about practice – practising weighing things up without any deeper meaning. Once you hit puberty, often those things that you feel embarrassed about, ashamed of, or guilty about in childhood equate to issues of low self-esteem and low self-worth in adulthood.

The rules can also be formed pretty easily by the significant adults in your childhood. If they have low self-worth, struggle with weight, are violent or abusive, or even suffer from depression and anxiety, then Rule Number 2, about things being connected to love, kicks in. It is not uncommon for me to see clients who are on a constant state of high alert because they were brought up by someone who worried about everything. A client who was hit or emotionally abused tends to be hyper-sensitive to other people's opinions of him and feels that he never measures up.

Social anxiety, a belief that you are not good enough, not lovable or likable can all stem from your subconscious trying to protect you from feeling left out of the pack. As ever, the way it often executes on this protection is to try and stop you engaging in those activities that will lead to you being hurt, which ironically then becomes the very thing that you feel bad about! For example:

You think: "I am not good enough to go for that promotion. Lots of people are more confident and outgoing than me, and I'd never get it anyway."

Your subconscious thinks: "If you go for the promotion and don't get it, then you will feel like you are not good enough, so the safest option is to not put yourself forward for stuff like that."

Your conclusion: "I'm useless. Why can't I be confident like other people and just try for stuff that I know I am capable of doing? The person who gets it probably won't be able to do it anywhere near as well as me."

The very thing your subconscious thinks it's protecting you from is usually the very thing that ends up happening.

I don't know about you, but I'm the sort of person that dwells on the stupid things I have done. I remember conversations, where I feel I said something stupid and embarrassing, for years afterwards. I replay it over and over again in my mind, groaning each time at how awful it was to say something or do something so totally embarrassing. I can even remember with great clarity stuff from my childhood where I was really embarrassed.

I once found myself in the headmaster's office at school when I was about ten. I had been given money every day to pay for school lunches, and instead of keeping the change somewhere safe and returning it to my mother at the end of the week, I went to the shops and bought sweets with it. I'm sure I had been doing this for a while when one day my mother asked me for the change, which of course I didn't have. Have you noticed how often children will out and out lie about something, which makes it way worse than if they confess early on and deal with the consequences? Even though my real mother never lifted a hand to me, I was scared, so instead of fessing up to what I had done, I lied. I told her I had lost the money. I thought that was the end of it and resolved to make sure I didn't spend the money on sweets in the future. Then the next day the headmaster called me into the office. Now, I was a very well behaved student, so I was even more scared at finding myself stood in front of the headmaster. He asked me if I had really lost the change. He told me that I should be honest if I hadn't lost it. I had already started the lie so I had to stick to it. I stood there physically shaking with fear and feeling my cheeks glow red as the temperature rose in my face. I was sure I was now in big trouble. He looked at me and then handed me some money. "You can tell your mum you found the change," he said, "and be very careful with it next time."

I left the office a wreck. I should have been elated that I had so cleverly managed to fool these adults, but the reality was that I was mortified that I had lied about this to two people now and been believed. I felt really guilty. As I write this down I still do and almost want to go back and pay back what was probably a very insignificant amount in loose change.

That event is only significant to my subconscious because of the need to fit in. I cheated the pack, and that felt very wrong. I have probably spent the rest of my life since over-compensating with too much honesty in a futile attempt to try and make up for it because it felt really bad. Your subconscious doesn't like stuff that makes you feel bad, so it puts stuff in the rulebook to try and protect you from that.

Jane's Story Revisited

If you remember from the last chapter, Jane has an emotional connection with the food she ate. But there were also issues there that related to self-esteem. She felt everyone was looking at her and thinking how fat she was. She couldn't stand to look at herself in the mirror. The problem was, the worse she felt about her failure to lose weight, the more she sought comfort from food, and the cycle was getting worse. Jane was binge eating on a regular basis which triggered a deep self-loathing, both for the weight it put on and the perceived lack of control she had over food and herself.

Jenny's Story – She Was Suffering Anxiety that Was So Bad She Had to Take Time Off Work

When circumstances changed at Jenny's work, she found herself experiencing an unfamiliar anxiety. The more often it happened, the worse it seemed to get, to the point where she no longer had any faith in her ability to do her job. Once the panic attacks started she had to go to her doctor, who signed her off work with stress and gave her anxiety medication. Each time she thought of going back she became more anxious until the doctor signed her off work with depression. Six months later she was trying a gradual return to work, but things were no better. She was worried she was going to lose her job which, despite everything, she loved. That's when she came to see me.

We Can't Read Minds

I know everyone thinks I'm stupid.

It's a common thing for my clients to say to me when they are suffering from anxiety and/or self-esteem issues. Note the "everyone" appearing again. When you are emotionally hijacked or in protection from something, you lose perspective, and small things become big, all-encompassing issues.

"You know?" I ask. "Can you read minds then? That's pretty cool if you can because I can't."

Of course no one says they can because you can't read minds. I certainly can't. Although a lot of people think because I am a Cognitive Hypnotherapist it means I can control minds. (I can't!) Even the famous magicians like Derren Brown, who give the appearance of being able to read minds, can't. They are just very clever at manipulating people's responses and reading body language.

Given that we all understand that mind-reading is technically not possible, it's amazing how many of us live our lives to meet our perceptions of what other people are thinking.

"When you are friends with someone," I sometimes ask my weight loss clients, "do you decide which ones you will be better friends with based on how they look? For example, if one of your friends wears a coat you don't like, will you refuse to talk to her that day? Or if another friend is fatter than you, does that mean you stay away from her?"

My clients look at me in horror at the very suggestion that they might judge people based on appearances, especially people they care about.

"So why do you think the people around you do that with you then?" I ask.

They are usually quiet at that point. It's such a ridiculous idea to think of doing that, and yet they are living their whole life assuming that other people are judging them. All because there is a caveman rule about the need to fit in, to feel part of a pack. And while there is a rational part of you that knows you are okay, the other part of you that is in control most of the time doesn't want you to believe that because it needs to protect you from getting hurt.

Some of this is a bit like not believing in God. I don't believe in God. In fact, I'm not really sure what I believe in. However, there is a little part of me that is really worried that if I shut the door to the possibility that God exists, something bad might happen if I'm wrong. I find it hard to say 100% I don't believe in God – just in case! When a client comes to see me with a belief that she is worthless, she tends to believe the opposite of worthlessness is arrogance. It isn't, of course. Being free from feeling that you are not good enough actually leaves you with the ability to make choices in your life that are right for you and your family, instead of being in protection mode. It allows you to grow and develop as a person. You are not suddenly going to become arrogant once you have the freedom to make those choices.

I can understand why it's really hard to understand that. After all, some clients have lived their whole lives defining themselves based on other people's opinions. How are they supposed to know who they are if they are looking at the world through filtered glasses? I read a phrase the other day: "We see the world not as it is but as we are." We all see colours in a unique way. We all taste food in a unique way.

I experienced this myself in my own journey. My childhood wasn't great. Okay, well, that's an understatement. It was pretty bad. Lots of people used the power they had over me in a way they really shouldn't have. As a result, by the time I survived all of that and was an adult, I felt I was pretty tough. I felt I didn't have to care what anyone else thought about me because I would never let anyone hurt me again. I felt my self-worth wasn't caught up in other people's opinions of me. So imagine my surprise when, in a therapy session, I was told that I needed to develop more iloc. In fairness, initially I had no idea what iloc was, so I read up on it. Iloc, it turns out, is internal locus of control.

Wikipedia defines this in a nice, simple way, I think:

Locus of control refers to the extent to which individuals believe that they can control events that affect them.

Understanding of the concept was developed by Julian B. Rotter in 1954, and has since become an aspect of personality studies. A person's "locus" (Latin for "place" or "location") is conceptualized as either internal (the person believes they can control their life) or external (meaning they believe that their decisions and life are controlled by environmental factors which they cannot influence).

I have to say I was confused. I wouldn't have said I had low self-worth, and I really didn't care what other people thought about me. However, I did believe that everyone was better than me. I did believe I was worthless and useless and not worth the air I breathed. (That does sound a bit like low self-worth doesn't it?) What I realised was, the belief that I was not good enough also allowed me to not take any responsibility for my actions. It allowed me to blame others for everything I couldn't do. Of course, it also meant I didn't take any credit for the stuff I could do, or did do, well. That stuff was just forgotten because it didn't fit the pattern of beliefs I had about myself.

In realising this, I also realised that actually my therapist was right. I believed my life was not in my control, not because of people in my present, but because of people from my past. I still allowed people who were in my past to have power over me. When I let go of that, I was able to take responsibility for my own actions and accept the consequences of my choices. I don't think I have ever felt more scared and lonely than I did for the few weeks after that realisation! There was no one else to blame. It was all me. Did everyone around me suddenly change after this realisation? Of course not, but I did. I was different. I looked at interactions differently. I realised that everything wasn't about me, and actually, the very thing that I had been protecting myself from was the very thing that was happening. I had believed that every person I met was judging me. That is arrogance, isn't it? To believe that you are so important to the people around you that their thoughts are taken up by you.

The reality is that we are all screwed up. In fact, we are so screwed up that we don't have time to think about other people because we spend all our time worrying what other people think about us. It's ironic really.

We can't read minds. And personally, I don't want to!

I once did some volunteer work with some troubled teenage girls. The organiser had an exercise that she did with each new group. She would draw a line on the ground and ask the girls to choose which side of the line they wanted to stand on. On one side they would have the power of invisibility, and on the other side was the ability to read minds. Which side do you think the majority of them chose? Which side would you choose? I know which side I would choose. I would go for the invisibility power. Almost all the girls, who were aged 14-15, chose the ability to read minds. This was because they cared so much what other people thought about them. This curse of caring so much what other people think, when you can't possibly know, tends to be underlying so many issues of low self-worth and low self-esteem.

I had a friend who was a lovely lady, very good at what she did. The problem was that she didn't believe she was as good as everyone else. Even when she had an opinion on something, she held back from offering it because she assumed others knew better than she and she was worried that she would look stupid. One day while we were chatting and swapping ideas, I was trying to encourage her to be more forthright in her opinion and believe in herself. The more I pushed, the more defensive she was becoming. I couldn't understand it. We had some great discussions, and she always had great ideas and great insight.

It became obvious that she had a Thing. She allowed me to help her find her Thing.

We went back to a time where she was ten years old. She had to go into a room in front of a panel of teachers and do a spelling test. She was doing fine until the fourth word out of ten when she spelt it wrong. They gave her a couple of chances to try again, but she had just developed a mental block and could not seem to get it right. The reason this became a problem for her subconscious was not that she couldn't spell that word. It wasn't even that the teachers sent her out of the room without even letting her attempt the other six words (which was very frustrating for her). It was that another girl in her class one she "knew" she was cleverer than, went in and scored ten out of ten. This other girl doing better than her when she hadn't even had the chance to try all the words was what hurt so much. In fact it hurt so much that it became a rule in her rulebook. She believed that she was not as clever as she thought she was, and that was not a nice feeling. It made her feel stupid. So her subconscious stuck a rule in her rulebook to protect her.

Do not speak out because it will make you look stupid and feel inadequate, and that will hurt.

The problem is, as is usually the case, the very thing that it was trying to protect her from was the thing she was feeling. Her lack of ability to speak out when she knew that her opinion was perfectly valid, and her frustration when other people said what she had been thinking and got recognised for it, made her feel stupid and inadequate. We changed the memory so that she was able to spell all ten words, and then she no longer had a problem with speaking out.

Closer Look: Jenny's Story
She was suffering anxiety that was so bad she had to take time off work.
Let's look again at Jenny who had started to experience such strong anxiety at work that she had been signed off by her doctor for months. Jenny didn't really understand what was going on because she'd always been competent at her work.

Initially I did a bit of pattern matching to see if there were times where she was okay with her skills and how that was different from the times where she doubted herself. She was fine until she got a new boss at work. Then the doubts had started to creep in about whether she was good enough. Her boss had pulled her up on a mistake she'd made, and then Jenny was determined that her boss had it in for her.

As we talked, it was clear that Jenny was filtering. Anything that reinforced her doubts and worries was given double the weight, and anything that reinforced that the boss was actually okay with the work she was doing was deleted. It was only as she was describing various situations to me that it became clear that it was her perspective and her external locus of control (believing her life, and the path of it, was in the control of her boss) was the thing that was causing the problem here, not anything specific that was actually happening.

It was clear that somehow, this new boss, and therefore new situation, had triggered a rule in her rulebook, and now I just needed to find the Thing. What was clear from her language was that the Thing related to not feeling she was good enough.

The problem with anxiety is that it doesn't really help you cope better right now because it takes your focus away from the present. We can't change what is in our past; we can't know what will happen in the future; all we can ever really do is appreciate what is happening right now. If you think about it, when has worrying about something ever really prepared you to deal with it better? And it's a bit crazy really; you worry about stuff that will happen in the future so you can better prepare yourself. You worry so you don't have to worry. You've got to love the way the subconscious works don't you?

For many years, I was very successful at work. I travelled the world consulting with businesses on how to improve the way they worked. I trained people, worked one on one, delivered presentations to senior management, talked to rooms filled with over a hundred people and did many other things that jet-setting global consultants do. I appeared confident and knowledgeable to the people around me. To a large degree I didn't care what the people around me thought about me because I had a secret. It wasn't really me! I was acting in a role; the role of confident, outgoing businesswoman. I was good at that role, but the real me, the one locked away safely inside, was riddled with anxiety. I just didn't allow her a voice, so it didn't get in the way of my life. But it did get in the way of my happiness.

I used to do this thing that I called Situation Thinking. It was my way of staying in control. I spent hours in my head working through all possible outcomes of the different situations I would be going into. Well, I say all possible outcomes, but really it was all the worst case scenarios. I would have a conversation with someone over and over again in my mind, rehearsing the way I could respond without giving away my feelings, no matter what they said. I firmly believed if I planned for the worst then I would be ready when it came. As a result, I lived my life with a deep underlying anxiety. I could never truly be happy because I ignored all the good stuff that was happening in the moment in favour of worrying about the future. I think the following quote sums it up nicely:

"Worry does not empty tomorrow of its sorrow. It empties today of its strength."
– *Corrie Ten Boom*

I was lucky because I found cognitive hypnotherapy and that all changed. Now I live in the moment and accept that what will be, will be. It's always my choice to take things in a way that maximises my happiness.

The Connection Between Caveman Rule Number 3 and Weight

While Caveman Rule Number 2 translates into eating to replace or dampen emotion, Caveman Rule Number 3 tends to lead to an abusive relationship with your body based on low self-esteem and confidence. Becoming aware that you might not be the same as everyone else can have significant negative implications to the way you see yourself. We are often so much more critical of ourselves than we would be of other people.

You do not see the world as it is, you see it as you are. You always have a choice on how you see things but you don't always realise it. Take the age-old question of whether you are an optimist or a pessimist. Are you a glass half-empty or a glass half-full person? I like to use this as a great example of having a choice in how you see things.

Someone hands me a glass filled to the halfway mark with cold water. I have two choices:

1. Be happy

"I have just been given half a glass of water, and I really wanted some water. How lucky am I to get what I want! I am going to really enjoy this cool, refreshing, drink of water."

2. Be unhappy

"Just my luck! I always get short changed on stuff. Why am I the one that gets only half a glass of water? There's hardly any point in bothering to drink it."

You always have a choice on how you see things. The fact is clear. There is a glass that is filled to the halfway point with water. What it means is a matter of choice and interpretation.

How does this relate to weight? I work with many clients who struggle with their weight, and weird thought this may sound, but I actually don't care how much weight someone loses. Who am I to decide what the right weight is for someone? Feeling like they look fat is purely a symptom of the individual's perception. Have you ever been in a room with friends and everyone has been talking about how much weight they have to lose? There is usually one of your friends, who has always been slim, talking about how she needs to lose a few pounds. You look at her and wish you were as slim as she was. I had a friend who went to a Zumba class and felt intimidated by the slim people in the class who were stood in front of the mirror watching themselves. She posted this on Facebook, and it was amusing how many people pointed out that they were probably looking in the mirror because they were unhappy with some aspect of their body and not, as she assumed, because they were admiring how good they looked. If a client decides to be happy as he is, I am just as thrilled as I am if he goes on to lose loads of weight. Both outcomes are true success because clients are free to choose.

I read the following in a compilation book edited by Steve Anderson called *Passing Time in the Loo* (Scarab Book LTD) and loved it. Unfortunately, I don't know to whom this story is attributed:

A gossip was complaining about a neighbour to a visiting friend. Her neighbour was so dirty, it was a disgrace to the neighbourhood. "Just look, those clothes she has on the line and sheets and pillowcases all have black streaks up and down them." Her guest said, "It appears, my dear, that the clothes are clean; the streaks you see are on your... windows."

You've heard of the term "rose-tinted glasses", meaning you see things as better than they are. Well, we all see things with glasses that filter stuff through our insecurities – through our own unique rulebook. Effectively you all have grimy windows unless you decide to clean them. We all probably have outfits that we think we look pretty good in, and others that we feel uncomfortable in even though they fit fine? Have you ever thought what it is that makes you feel different in the different outfits?

Think of someone who is suffering from anorexia. The person looks in the mirror and sees fat. In the worst case she deprives herself so much that she dies of starvation, all because what she sees, through her filtered glasses, is a fat person. This is something very different to what friends and family see when they look at her. The reasons that lead her to that perception will almost certainly stem from one or more of The Caveman Rules.

The good news, if you accept this to be true (and all my evidence of working with clients suggest it is), you can choose to see things differently. However, first you need to clear the trigger for protection out of the way.

Having a problem with your size and the way you look is all about fitting in. So what are some of the reasons that your subconscious thinks it's a good idea to keep weight on even when you consciously don't want it?

- If you keep the weight on then people will judge you for weight instead of your personality, and it's a lot easier to believe that someone doesn't like you because you are fat than because you are not a nice person.

- Being overweight gives you an excuse not to take part in activities that might require you to mix with people you don't know. Mixing with people you don't know makes you feel inferior/inadequate.

- Being overweight stops you being attractive (in your mind!) and stops unwanted attention (Caveman Rule Number 1 or 2).

A question that you can ask yourself is: "If there was no one around who could judge me or see me, would I still be unhappy with my size?" Issues of weight are rarely purely to do with just feeling too big. There is almost always something in there to do with the way you identify yourself as a fat person and what being fat means. I use the word "fat" for explanation purposes because I think it is a judgement word in itself and not a word I would use to describe anyone. Who am I to know what is fat versus slim versus overweight? And in fact, I really don't care. But my clients usually do.

I was in a restaurant with my daughter when she was five. There was a little girl across the table from us that looked a year or two older than my daughter and was definitely chubbier than other girls of her age. My daughter said, "Look at the fat girl over there." I called my daughter over to me, horrified to hear her utter such a thing. The joy of having to send your children to school is that they pick up stuff you would never teach them. We never use the word fat in our house and, while we might joke about our big tummies after we have had a meal, we don't draw attention to any flaws we believe we have with our body (and trust me, I need therapy as much as the next person on that one!). I started lecturing her on how you should never, ever refer to anyone as fat. I told her that she should always try and avoid describing someone based on the way they look, unless you need to pick them out of a crowd.

She looked at me and said, "Mummy, what does fat mean?"

Ah ha! It's easy to forget children use words they don't understand. I explained that technically it means the layer of white stuff under the skin that keeps us warm. I went on to explain that calling someone fat means different things to different people. To some it's a really mean thing to say and would really upset them, and others wouldn't care. In our house we try very hard not to be mean and not to upset people. In fact, if we are going to have an impact on anyone around us, it is to make them happy. So we agreed that we would never refer to anyone as fat again, and in fairness, she has stuck to that pretty well.

Closer Look: Jane's Story

She'd tried every diet and was desperate to lose the weight.

Let's look at Jane again, who had tried every diet going and was desperate to lose the weight. She believed she had terrible willpower because she couldn't stick to a diet. She always put the weight back on. It was a relief to her to know that it was really just normal behaviour, and it really wasn't her fault. She felt everyone was looking at her and thinking how fat she was. She couldn't stand to look at herself in the mirror. The problem was that the worse she felt about her failure to lose weight, the more she sought comfort from food, and the cycle was getting worse. Jane was binge eating on a regular basis, which triggered a deep self-loathing both for the weight it put on and the perceived lack of control she had over food and herself.

There clearly were issues to do with self-esteem as well as an emotional connection to food. This is often the case with clients. I usually find it takes some work to get through the layers, starting with the emotional behaviour around food, and then once you have sorted that, you can begin to work on the issues with the way they see themselves.

Jane had lost weight in the past, but the minute she started to feel slim she felt she sabotaged herself and put it all back on again – and then some! Jane felt like a failure. As we talked, it became clear that this was the Thing at the root of her problems losing weight.

I ask all weight loss clients what size they would like to be. I don't work with pounds and kilos because if someone decides to tone up, then they will put weight on. Also, who really wants to lose weight so they can wander round with the scales and show people how much they weigh now? People want to lose weight because they want to look and feel different. Once they have answered "I want to be a size X", I ask two more questions: "Why not size X+1 or size X-1?" This allows me to see where their perception of the size they want to be really comes from. Sometimes they don't want to be a smaller size (X-1) because they don't think it's realistic. Sometimes they don't want to be bigger size (X+1) because that doesn't match their idea of what a slim person should look like. This can give an insight into where their self-image comes from – a parent, kids at school, etc.

I then ask, "And if I told you that you had to stay the size you are right now, what would that mean?" Sometimes they cry when I ask this question. The sense of failure to be "stuck" where they are can be very upsetting. And that tells me something. From these questions I can understand what the source of the Thing is likely to be.

Jane did not want to be the fat mother at the school gates. Each day when she took her daughter to school, she would wait in the car because she didn't want the other mothers talking about how fat she was. She hadn't been able to take her daughter swimming because she wouldn't be seen in a swimming costume. It was getting in the way of her life. She wanted to lose four dress sizes, and she thought that would make her confident enough to fit in with the other mothers.

The reason she chose the size she wanted to get to was because that's the size she was when she was a teenager. In discussion, she talked about how she always felt fat, but now when she looks back at photos of her younger self, she realises she wasn't fat at all, and she wishes she was that size now. She has never felt slim.

If I helped Jane lose weight without doing anything else, she would most probably still be unhappy. She was not able to accept that her appearance wasn't the most important thing. She couldn't see that her daughter, her husband and her friends loved her for who she was and didn't care about her looks and especially not her size. She couldn't see that because it mattered so much to her that every comment and every inter-action was getting translated into a problem with her weight.

The Boy/Girl Issue

While issues with the way you see yourself tend to be more common if you are a woman, men are also very much affected by this caveman rule. In my experience, in men it tends to result in anxiety around fitting in more than a weight related appearance issues.

Let's look back again at the roles of men and women in caveman days. The caveman was the hunter gatherer. His place in the pack was strongest when he was a good hunter and could feed the clan. The stronger he was, the stronger his place was in the pack. It was important for him to have children, but only in the same way as people like to breed from good racehorses or greyhounds – they are good stock and so should have good offspring. If the caveman was too slow or lacked the skills necessary to throw a spear, then he was a liability and would be left out, or get killed during the hunt.

These days the prowess of a male is not measured by his ability to hunt, but men who are strong and athletic are generally regarded as more attractive than men who appear weak physically and are more brain than brawn. Politicians and men in positions of power are more likely to draw attention from women, irrespective of what they look like. No matter what you consciously think, a woman's subconscious is attracted to the man that more fits the caveman definition of strong!

The thing is, while your subconscious works on The Caveman Rules, consciously women would prefer to be with a man who is an equal partner. She doesn't want clubbing over the head and dragging about by her hair (or the modern day equivalent which is being left at home with expectations that she will cook, clean, raise children and do nothing else)! In our society these days, attraction isn't about who can throw the furthest spear or run faster. Men don't generally gather together to show off their skills to attract a mate. (Getting your hair just right so you look your best when you go out clubbing doesn't count as a skill I'm afraid!)

Competitions where athleticism and strength are showcased like the Olympics now include both men and women. Connections are made in lots of different ways, but most often it begins with a conversation, not a show of skills. Your minds connect before your bodies do. Malcolm Gladwell explains, in his book *Blink*, how it is the first ten seconds or so where you form an opinion of a person. Instant attraction is governed by a spark, but turning the spark into a longer burning flame is down to something more significant than instant physical attraction.

When growing up, this rule means that a boy is just as likely as a girl to suffer from self-esteem issues if they feel like they don't fit in. Remember, the pack mentality applies when you are in or out of the pack, so a pack will single out someone who is weak in caveman terms. While a girl will be most likely to take this as an issue with the way she looks (we will discuss this in a moment) and so can self-sabotage to make herself less attractive (perception not reality!), a boy tends to have fewer options in terms of what they do when they are singled out as the weakest in a pack. For boys, a subconscious perception of not fitting in rarely equates to their looks. It equates to them not being fit to support the pack. It means they are useless, and therefore it fundamentally affects their self-worth. In my opinion this is why so many teenage boys commit suicide, or even worse, take a shotgun into their school and kill teachers and other children.

As an adult it can lead to feelings of inadequacy and low self-worth. Men who have been bullied as children are likely to try to keep themselves out of society as much as possible and suffer from lengthy bouts of depression. The risk of suicide may stay with them throughout their adult life, even when they have a family and successful career.

So how about the cavewoman? Her role was to keep the clan alive. This is both in feeding and clothing and also in breeding. Her role was to ensure there were future generations to continue the legacy. This meant the critical qualities of a cavewoman centred on attractiveness to a mate, and success at producing and bringing up offspring.

These days, attractiveness remains the single most important "measure of success" in being a woman. While women no longer need to remain indoors cooking, cleaning and breeding, everything is still geared towards appearance. In my years in business I had at least three managers who gave me specific feedback indicating I should power-dress if I wanted to be more successful. Power-dress was obviously wearing a skirt suit and not trousers and a jacket like I chose to do. The feedback on my performance in various roles was consistently excellent, but somehow it still mattered that I conformed to an acceptable female dress code if I wanted to be truly successful.

Everything with a woman is about appearance because everything about being a successful cavewoman was about being attractive. As a woman you can consciously choose not to care, but that only applies to the 10% of the day where you are in control; for the other 90% you are working to The Caveman Rules.

When something happens during childhood that results in a girl feeling unattractive, then a rule can go into a rulebook to protect her from how bad that feels. It can trigger a series of steps in a weird sort of back-to-front way to sabotage her attractiveness. For example, she may turn to food for comfort. There is certain logic to this. It can be so painful to think you are innately unattractive that you subconsciously take action to make yourself deliberately unattractive by eating. Weight can also be an effective way of hiding a feminine shape – like a protective suit – which means that you get less attention and can stay below the radar. After all, if you make yourself unattractive, then you don't need to worry about competing with those other girls that you believe will always beat you. The other thing girls tend to do more than boys (although boys sometimes do this too) is self-harm. There are many different reasons for self-harming, and there are many different ways of doing it. It can be a tool to hurt a body you hate. It can also be a mechanism to turn emotional pain into physical pain that you can see and watch as it heals. Whichever way it comes out, if a girl feels she doesn't fit in because of her looks, then often her way to address this as an adult can be to sabotage her looks.

So this caveman rule really does apply equally to boys and girls but for different reasons and different adult behaviour as a consequence.

Getting Rid of the Trigger

As with the other two rules, the key to moving on from this is to find the Thing and then work out what the rule in the rulebook is. By deleting the rule from the rulebook you are free to move on with your life, free from the pesky trigger that has been driving behaviour you don't want.

The Solution: Jenny's Story
She was suffering anxiety that was so bad she had to take time off work.
Let's look again at Jenny who started to experience such strong anxiety at work that when she went to the doctor, he gave her a sick note so she could be off work for three months. I had discovered that her Thing was related to not feeling she was good enough and that, now she had a new boss, she was going to be found out.

Now all I needed to do was find out where that came from. When we went on a Thing hunt, we found an event when she was outside the school gates with a group of friends. One of the friends was her best friend. Her friend had been through a lot, and she'd made a point of being there for her through it all. Yet she found herself on this day, when she was about fourteen years old, being picked on by some of the other girls. Instead of standing up for her, her best friend joined in. To her subconscious this was the ultimate evidence of not fitting in.

She was outside of the pack, and that hurt. It hurt even more because her best friend, part of her mini-pack, was in with the pack.

The emotions of this memory were still strong as she looked down on it, so it was a bit tricky to get her to step back and look at it from an adult perspective. The trick to getting over this caveman rule is to realise that it doesn't matter what other people think of you. Also, it helps to realise that everyone is screwed up in some way shape or form. Teaching her to become an observer and see how that situation was actually not about her, but the other people in it, was the key to getting rid of the rule. I helped her to take the box off her head. When she did she realised a couple of things: her friend had never really been a good friend to her, and she'd used her and given little back to the friendship. She also realised the other girls that were picking on her were not the ones she even wanted to be friends with. She was only there because of her "best" friend. She realised that everyone wants to fit in, and they were all behaving in a way that they believed would make them fit in best.

Having begun to appreciate that (and remember you can't un-see something once you have seen it), then the next important thing to do was to get her to be able to appreciate some of the qualities that she had as a person – qualities that would allow her to begin to let go of needing external validation for what she did – qualities that would allow her to be okay with who she was and is now. The full acceptance of this would take time, but in this moment we had an opportunity to get things started. I asked her, as an adult, to think of some of her good qualities. She was able to think about what a good friend she had been. She could see that it was because of her loyalty and friendship that she had felt to betrayed. She was able to see that she was caring and resilient. Then it was simply a matter of passing all the knowledge and learning down to the fourteen-year-old version of herself so she could let go of it once and for all. She changed the moment and simply walked away from them all. She did it with a smile on her face because she had also passed down the hindsight about where the other girls would end up. Clearly, as adults, they had not been as successful as her. That helped a lot!

The beauty of this approach is that you fundamentally change the triggers of the thoughts, feelings and behaviours, which means that there is no conscious need to counter them when they come up. They simply won't come up any more. When Jenny went back to work she realised that the boss didn't actually have any problem with her. In fact, the boss valued her work so much that she was putting her forward for projects with more responsibility to progress her career. Prior to our session Jenny assumed that her boss was setting her up for failure. After our session she saw it for what it was: a sign of faith in her skills and capabilities.

The Solution: Jane's Story
She tried every diet and was desperate to lose the weight.
Let's look at Jane again, who had tried every diet going and was desperate to lose the weight. She believed she had terrible willpower because she couldn't stick to a diet. She always put the weight back on. It was a relief to her to know that it was really just normal behaviour and it really wasn't her fault. She felt everyone was looking at her and thinking how fat she was. She couldn't stand to look at herself in the mirror. Jane's Thing was that her perception of how she looked was warped by her own fears.

When looking for the rule in Jane's rulebook, I wanted to find the first event that was connected with her being unhappy with how she looked. Kids are not naturally self-conscious. One of the things I enjoy most about my daughter is that she will choose what to wear and will wear the craziest combinations because she likes it, not because she cares what other people think. Caring what other people think is about fitting into the pack. What I knew for sure with Jane is that there would be a moment that made her conscious of how she looked in comparison to others.

As an aside here, when the slimming clubs started up here in the UK, people would go along once a week or so to get weighed and told off or praised by the group leader. This sort of public accountability was quite new for us Brits, and it caused quite a lot of anxiety. People would be very "good" for the few days before their weigh-in, and then after they would give themselves a treat (no matter what the result) by having their dinner out. It was not uncommon for a woman to take her daughter along once they were about eight years old or more, and then both of them would follow the programme once back home.

This created a household where how much fat, or how many calories, something contained was a common discussion (as was how fat someone looked). This primed the child or children in the household to be constantly thinking about how much they ate and how they looked at an age when it shouldn't really matter because their shape was changing all the time. I have seen many clients whose problems with their self-image, and difficult relationship with food, was established because a well-meaning mother put them on a diet at an early age.

So when we asked Jane's subconscious to take us to the first event connected to her becoming aware of her shape and size being something she was unhappy with, it took us back to when she was thirteen years old and getting changed after gym class at school. She was looking around at the other girls and noticed she had bigger hips than them. This made her feel that there was something wrong with her. It made her feel that she wasn't as attractive as the other girls (even though that's not what she was consciously thinking).

Again this is a fairly common thing for me to hear. At an age when a girl is going through puberty her body is not changing at an even and balanced rate. We are all unique, and it is, unfortunately, perfectly normal to compare ourselves to those around us. To correct the connection that her subconscious had made to this observation and Jane's self-esteem, it was once more just a matter of lifting the box off her head. Jane was a mother, and this can be powerful for a number of reasons. Firstly, bigger hips when you are a mum is a good thing; it is a very primal sign of success in having babies – "child-bearing hips". So she could see, with an adult perspective, that what she saw in that moment as a bad thing that made her stand out, was actually the thing that had made it easier for her to be a mother. Her "child bearing hips" had carried her much-loved daughter. The other thing about being a mother is that when you are trying to reframe something you can get the client to imagine what she would say to her child in the same situation. She is rarely going to be as judgemental and cruel to her own child as she is to herself. And finally we shared the benefit of hindsight. Letting her thirteen-year-old self see how the shapes of the other girls changed as they grew older, and also how her shape changed, allowed her to let go of the belief that there was anything wrong with it.

Shifting her perspective, allowing her to see that we are all different and there was nothing wrong with her at that age, allowed her to let go of the belief that she didn't fit in.

In accepting her shape and size she was now free to choose to be whatever size she wanted to be without it being an emotional thing. She was free to choose to eat healthily, exercise more and as a result was able to lose the weight at a steady rate that was permanent without having to resort to any extreme steps, like diets where all you eat is the food that is sent to you or even a gastric band (fitted either hypnotically or physically).

Fooling the Child – Flip It!

Bringing up a child with the resilience to understand that stuff isn't about him is probably one of the trickiest tasks, mainly because it is something most adults don't get either. How can you possibly teach your child that it doesn't matter what people think of him when you've spent your whole life believing the opposite?

As adults, we can have lots of layers of protection based on our experiences as a child. However, if you really think about it, would you want your child to feel the same way that you do? Or would you instead want them to be able to appreciate all the wonderful qualities they have and not care what other people think about them? I suspect the latter. By now you should realise we always have a choice in how we see things.

Imagine if your child (or children) could grow up to be the sort of person that didn't have to change his behaviour based on any perceptions of what other people think. This is not about being wild and out of control; of course there are rules in society that you have to follow. This is instead about being whoever you want to be instead of constantly trying to protect yourself from being hurt.

To learn how to shift perspective, when something hurts you or makes you feel defensive, try a task I call "Flip It". In any inter-action – email, phone call, meeting in person – ask the following question:

If this was not about me, but instead about something going on in another person's head, what might it be about?

Here are some examples from my clients:

- I thought while cooking a roast that my parents wouldn't like it compared to the way my mother cooked it. But then I flipped it to realise that her cooking is not superior to mine, just different. Actually I was really looking forward to my own cooking, and for us, it was going to be better than my mum's roast earlier in the week.

- I flipped my mother's comment about me being ready for a break from my daughter; it's not personal about me, my daughter or my parenting skills. It is about any parent with a two-year-old full time, or even how my mum felt when I was that age.

- I was getting annoyed by people's social media sharing of "fight the lard" when they are a size twelve. I was taking it like it was personal against all fat people. I flipped it to realise that most people, whatever their size, are critical of themselves and may feel that they are bigger than they want to be. I should be happy for their exercise and healthy eating.

Once you have perfected this, you can teach your children to think the same way.

Trauma – The Exception to the Rulebook

There is a situation where the rulebook and the rules of survival are not followed because it would actually hinder survival. This is when you experience trauma.

So what is trauma? People often only think of trauma as being the result of a wartime situation such as seeing someone blown up, or even being caught up in a terrorist situation where a bomb has gone off nearby. In my experience any event can be treated by the brain as traumatic. It's the impact on your mind that defines whether it's a trauma or not.

Wikipedia states:

> Psychological trauma is a type of damage to the psyche that occurs as a result of a severely distressing event.
>
> A traumatic event involves a single experience, or an enduring or repeating event or events, that completely overwhelm the individual's ability to cope or integrate the ideas and emotions involved with that experience. The sense of being overwhelmed can be delayed by weeks, years or even decades, as the person struggles to cope with the immediate circumstances.

It may not surprise you that this pattern still relates to the caveman brain.

When you experience a traumatic situation, the subconscious can enter a fairly intense protection-mode that, while based on the caveman principles, does not come from the rulebook. In this situation, to react emotionally would be too much. You actually need to disengage your emotional response and use cool, calm thought to increase your chances of survival and to stop your mind from "breaking". To do this, your subconscious shuts down the emotional part and enhances the cognitive part of your brain.

This is not an instant process. It takes time for your mind to experience the effect of what has happened, attempt to rationalise and cope with it, and then, if necessary, identify the best way to protect you in the future. It is a complex and unpredictable process that requires full engagement from mind and body. As with any of The Caveman Rules, a traumatic event for one person may not even register with someone else.

If there is any caveman rule this relates to it's the first one – react first. This is about survival at a very basic level. While there is a physical response, it is not to get you ready for a fight or to run away. In the case of trauma this instant physical response needs to be supressed.

If trauma requires that you engage a cognitive rather than emotional process, what is the role of the subconscious? After all, the subconscious is in charge for at least 90% of the day so it must have a part to play.

Let's look at it in caveman terms for a moment to see if we can understand it better. The mind is programmed to keep you alive no matter what. To do this it depends on an ability to pattern match and apply rules – the three caveman rules of survival. But what happens if something so extreme happens that not only does not fit any patterns, but it also means you need to take instant evasive action? It is not enough to simply enter a rule in the rulebook. The normal day to day stuff of fighting sabre-toothed tigers, hunting and protecting your clan, were unlikely to cause trauma.

If there was an unusual event, such as seeing your entire clan savaged by a sabre-toothed tiger, then that's a whole different ball game. Your natural instinct might cause you to freak out and run away, but this would put you at risk. You need to be able to shut down the fight, flight or freeze response and remain calm. You need to be able to think rather than react, which is the opposite of how it normally goes. This requires quite a significant powering down of the emotional system to stop it taking over. It requires the creation of a sort of protective black hole. With the emotions now safely out of the way, you are now in a position to take the best action for survival. The action you take in trauma is the opposite of what you would normally do because that is how you survive. The rulebook is irrelevant. As a caveman, survival of the clan in this situation would be dependent on you surviving at all costs. You need to be able to deal with checking the members of your clan, once the sabre-toothed tiger has gone, to see if you can save any of them. You need to gather your supplies, and you need to keep going for long enough to find another clan to attach to. You cannot afford to take the time to feel sorry for yourself or upset.

Back to the modern day, while a traumatic event may have no obvious connection to survival, once your brain has triggered that protective shutdown, then the net effect of the trauma is the same. This can be triggered by an overwhelming emotional trauma that is too profound to process or a physical event leading to an overwhelming emotional response. This type of trauma event can happen at any point in a person's life because it is independent of the rulebook. In effect it's a rule unto itself. To prevent the emotional impact of trauma taking over, which will limit your capacity to survive, the solution is to cut off the emotion. For the duration of the need to cope with the impact of the traumatic event, the emotions need to remain shut off.

Consider a situation where a ferry capsizes. Survival is usually dependent on instinctive reaction. Most people will have no experience or training that prepares them for the right action to take when they are trapped in a sinking boat. The natural fear response will be fight, flight or freeze. If the subconscious leads a person to their instinctive reaction at this point, the chances of survival are limited. What is really required is the ability to evaluate different escape routes, work out if there is enough air, decide who you can help, etc. This is the role of the prefrontal cortex which is normally switched off when you are in protection mode. The people with the best chance of surviving will be the ones who can enter a zone where the emotion is gone and cool, calm rational thinking takes over. These are the people who don't go into a caveman trance driven by the rules of survival but rather think their way out of the situation.

The catch here is that the brain is way too complex to just isolate a particular circuit with no other consequences. To begin with, the initial trauma has already started a psychological and physiological chain reaction. You know already that the mind and body are linked. In the same way as the mind informs the body, the body informs the mind, so simply breaking the connection can leave the body frustrated because it isn't being listened to. This leaves a build-up of energy in the body with nowhere to go which may eventually begin to take a physical toll on your organs. It may just come out as shaking initially, but a number of other things like a weakened immune system, or an increase in blood pressure as a result of increased adrenaline may be going on at the same time.

Generally, those who have studied trauma say it is likely to create an emotional numbness initially, which makes sense if you consider the need to survive. Emotions get in the way. It is also why you should leave it for weeks or even months before you attempt to treat the effects of a trauma because it may be that the brain won't go into shutdown and survive mode after all. We are all unique, so what one person takes as traumatic is not the same as someone else. The next phase, if trauma has in fact been regis-tered, is likely to be an emotional and physical reaction which can be characterised by changes in behaviour. The symptoms may include:

- Vivid flashbacks either consciously while awake or in the form of nightmares. These flashbacks may often be triggered by things that remind you of the traumatic event. This can be sights, sounds or even smells.

- Emotional numbness as an ongoing form of protection. You may also find yourself turning to a substance to cope with the emotions if the numbness hasn't kicked in. This can lead to addictions and depression.

- An unsettling lack of structure in your post-trauma brain. You might find you are quicker to anger or even rage, easily panicked or often anxious. You might find that you feel detached which can lead to feeling out of place and depressed.

In order to allow you to function despite trauma, what your brain has to do is get rid of the rulebook. Not only does it not help with survival in the case of a traumatic situation, but it actually hinders it. Following the rules for survival, depending on instinct, and protecting yourself from being hurt have no place when you just have to survive no matter what. So the rulebook gets buried. It is locked away somewhere in your brain, and along with it go all the things that keep you safe and secure. All the familiar patterns that you are used to following. All the things that have helped you understand how to interact with the world since you became an adult – all locked away. This can leave you in a state of hyper-vigilance where you are evaluating each of the cavemen rules in real-time, with no established lessons on how to interpret them. Everything is a bigger risk. Nothing is safe.

This is all well and good while the traumatic event is ongoing, but what happens after? Does the brain know to go and fetch the rulebook back? The answer is no, not in my experience. In my experience the problem with a traumatic event is that the rulebook remains locked away after. What this means is that you end up having to apply The Caveman Rules for Survival in their raw form with no guidance on what they mean for you. This can mean people become overly anxious about every situation, even ones where they used to be fine, because they don't know what will and won't hurt them anymore (Caveman Rule Number 1). Everything is a potential threat. It can also lead to depression as a person may feel increasingly isolated, feeling that contact with other people is not safe (Caveman Rule Number 3). Without a rulebook you don't have a framework for survival.

When I see clients, sometimes it isn't obvious that there is a trauma in their past or even that a particular event has registered as traumatic. It really depends on when the traumatic event happened. The earlier it happened in their life, the trickier it can be. Sometimes I find a blank spot when I talk to a client – a place you are not allowed to look. Or sometimes there is a Thing, an elephant in the room that they won't talk about. We will dance around dealing with other stuff, and I might be confused that the client doesn't experience the scale of change I would normally expect. If I'm lucky, I develop a good enough relationship with my client, and they will pluck up the courage to let me know what's going on. It takes a significant amount of courage to open your head up to someone else and "confess" to a traumatic event. With most therapeutic approaches you need to reveal what the trauma was to be able to work on it; with cognitive hypnotherapy you don't. All the work is done in the client's head with my guidance.

If a traumatic event happens in childhood it might not be obvious that it even exists. In my experience the subconscious protects these memories as much as it can. While they might affect the client's behaviour, until you re-programme the emotional impact of the event, neither the client, nor the therapist, may have any idea which behaviours and beliefs were a result of the shutdown versus which were innate to the personality. When the rulebook is locked away before it has been completed, then a client may have no idea who they truly are. It can be a very scary journey!

The rulebook doesn't go away though. For an adult that has been trauma-free most of his life, there is a robust rulebook that is tucked away somewhere safe. It's possible to look into it, but the emotional significance of anything in there is limited by guard dog channels that don't let the emotions out any more. Remember, with trauma, emotions are not safe.

The trick with dealing with trauma is to clear out this defensive barrier, the guard dogs, and re-establish two-way communication with the emotional part of the brain and the part of the brain where the rulebook sits.

Most people are aware of trauma that comes out of horrific experience in combat, accidents like plane crashes and boat crashes or even a sexual assault. It even has a term: "PTSD" or Post-Traumatic Stress Disorder. While there are now many approaches to dealing with PTSD, most focus on helping someone rebuild her life post-trauma. I focus on removing the short circuit in the brain that was created by the trauma, which then allows the brain to return to a "normal" way of working.

Often people aren't aware that the trauma response can be triggered by a whole range of different events. Experiencing intense negative emotion can make an event traumatic. It doesn't have to be the result of an event that happened in your environment.

Birth Trauma

Birth can often be a traumatic experience for a woman. There can be a combination of pain, exposure, vulnerability and even humiliation. This is not a good combination for a brain that is trying to keep you alive. Due to the nature of labour and giving birth, there is also no escape, and this can be exaggerated when giving birth in hospital. When something goes wrong there is quite a high risk of trauma. The thing is, as all women who have children have to go through the process of labour and giving birth, there seems to be an unwritten rule in society that you should be able to cope – a rule that says no matter what happens, it is all part of the process, and if you complain or make out that it was tough in any way, then you are weak and inadequate. This, of course, isn't true. But it is a belief carried by many women who have experienced complications in birth that have resulted in being traumatised.

This trauma can be one of the triggers leading to post-natal depression (PND). Depression is one of those mental health conditions that is already kept quiet by most people, so you add the layer of "just deal with it" that is implied by childbirth, and it can lead to lethal consequences. A woman who experiences PND, who attempts suicide, usually does it in a violent way which is not typical for women; outside of PND women tend to favour less violent forms of suicide, such as an overdose. There is also a belief that PND is a condition experienced by women only when their baby is young. However, I have come across clients with PND when their children are between eight and twelve years old. Once triggered, the depressive state can stay with a woman for life.

I have worked with a number of women who came to see me about a problem such as anxiety, depression or general self-esteem issues who had experienced some sort of trauma during childbirth. Clearing the trauma, by disconnecting the emotion from the memory, has generally gone a long way towards clearing the other problems.

Elizabeth's Story – A Traumatic Birth

Elizabeth came to see me for various reasons. Most of the reasons were wrapped up in self-esteem. She wanted to lose weight, she was constantly worried about upsetting people, and she wanted to be a better mother to her young son with whom she was really struggling.

Over the period of three sessions we dealt with each of her Things and progress was good in many areas. Her confidence had improved a lot, and she was finding that she was beginning to enjoy time with her son instead of dreading it.

But weirdly the weight just would not shift. Nothing we did seemed to make a difference. In fact, while she was doing really well at completing tasks I gave her for the other stuff, she wasn't doing any of the tasks I gave her for her weight. She wouldn't practise mindful eating. She didn't listen to the weight loss MP3 download I gave her, instead favouring the earlier downloads that related to confidence. She wouldn't do anything for herself and felt that the therapy just wasn't working. Yet she kept coming back to see me.

In our fourth session I was doing some more digging to find out when the weight had really become a problem for her, and she started talking about the birth of her son. The minute she started recalling the birth, she started crying. She could not tell me anything about why. It seemed just the thought of sharing what had happened was causing her to panic. I could tell that her birth experience had been traumatic. It became clear why nothing we did was really sticking. We weren't fully engaging with her subconscious in each session. We were seeing the root of the problem, the Thing, but there was a protected communication channel back to it so no matter what we did to show the subconscious that something was just a miscalculation, it was not having the emotional impact I would expect.

When I recognised what was going on I explained to Elizabeth that her brain had registered her birth experience as traumatic and that it had been protecting her ever since. She was visibly relieved. She thought she was just making a big deal over nothing.

So I set to removing the defensive barrier around the trauma. The beauty of the approach I use is that it is all done by the client. I didn't need to know a single detail of what actually happened to help free her up from her prison. This is particularly significant when a client has a traumatic memory. There is a reason why it's traumatic, and the last thing they want to do is share it!

It took no more than ten minutes to clear the trauma from the memory. The memory of the birth and the details of it remained fully intact. It was the emotional dimension that changed. As we finished the session she was smiling. She was able to talk about the birth without any tears. In time she was even able to entertain the idea of having more kids – something that terrified her before our session.

Even better, getting rid of the guard dogs allowed access to her rulebook with a two-way communication once more, and the work we had already done, and the downloads she already had, began to take effect, and the weight started to come off.

Childhood Trauma

Another trigger for the brain to kick off a trauma response can happen through childhood abuse. This is a particularly tricky one to clear because once you have cleared the trauma, you are unlikely to have a complete rulebook to return to as a default. It simply would not have been written at the point of the trauma.

While childhood abuse can happen for a prolonged period of time, it is unlikely to be the totality of the time spent being abused that caused the trauma reaction in the brain. There is probably one, or maybe two or three moments in the abuse that tipped that balance between the normal coping and survival mechanism to a level of intolerable emotional intensity that required an emotional shutdown.

There are many tricky things about dealing with this kind of trauma. Firstly, there are your perceptions of what is traumatic. I have heard some horrific stories of things done to children – things that I shudder to think of, and am in awe that someone is able to get through that kind of stuff. But that is down to the way I see the world, and you can't possibly know what an experience is like unless you have been through it yourself. The human capacity to endure and survive is phenomenal.

Secondly, the client may not be aware that something has actually been categorised as traumatic. In fact it may be a blank area that they are either not allowed near, or when they try to look, they see nothing. The first clue that you have may be a resistance to "going there" when you are working on some other aspect of their problem.

Thirdly, the subconscious may be doing such a good job of protecting that area and that person that you simply are not allowed to attempt to do anything. The fear of opening Pandora's Box may prevent you from being allowed to try. The alternative of living with the symptoms may be less scary.

Fourthly, what do you do when you have cleared the trauma? How do you recreate a rulebook that doesn't even exist? And recognising that you probably can't, how do you fill the void that is left behind after you have removed the trauma short-circuit?

Peter's Story – An Abused Child

Peter hated himself. He hated everything about his life and frequently considered suicide, but there was something stopping him actually going through with it. Peter had spent his life trying to find the thing that would free him up from his pain. He came to me, as so many people do, as a last ditch attempt. After me, he was going to give up trying.

Peter had a very abusive childhood covering physical, emotional and sexual abuse. As with any of my clients, I only needed minimal details to be able to help him move forward. The problem was, any foray into his childhood would lead to a severe abreaction. An abreaction is different for everyone, but it is caused by a battle between the conscious and subconscious over a traumatic experience. The way Peter "did" his abreaction was to shake violently. The only thing he would say was "don't know", and he would stare at a fixed spot intently. Our early sessions were about tiptoeing around this space and trying to get small changes – to build the trust.

Then one day, at the start of the session, he told me he couldn't go on like this anymore. He wanted to stop having that reaction and be able to feel good enough to move on with his life. He felt that despite all the changes, he couldn't ever feel okay with this black thing hanging over him.

I explained that what I was about to do would all happen in his head and that he wouldn't need to tell me a single detail. I also explained that, while at the start it would be really unpleasant, it would not be any worse than what he is living with every day, and on the other side it would be significantly better.

I then asked if there was a particularly memory that kept running in his head, almost like a video clip. When something is traumatic there is usually something like this right at the front of the subconscious mind. It is a constant video clip looping on repeat. It is no different whatever the cause of the trauma. It applies whether the trauma was a short-term or a long-term experience; there will still always be that moment that tipped the balance away from following the "traditional" rules of survival.

He had no difficulty finding it, and I could see that just accessing that memory was already sending him towards abreaction. Normally I get my client to engage with the memory until the intensity is at least eight out of ten, but I could see from his reaction that we just needed to get started. Early on his whole body was tense, and it was hard for me to ask him to keep replaying the video clip. I only kept going because I knew it would be worth it. Eventually, after what felt like hours but was really only around fifteen minutes, we finished cycling round, and when I asked him how intense the feeling was, he shrugged his shoulders and said "about a two…".

I provided him with an MP3 download to listen to daily

after our session. When I saw him a couple of months later he was a changed man. He held himself with a confidence I had not seen before and had a new philosophy: "What will be, will be." He was also starting to consider his future and things he would like to do – something unheard of when I first met him.

There is nothing you can do to prevent a traumatic situation from happening. What may be taken as a trauma by one person may not even register with someone else. For this reason, you need to be cautious when working with someone who has experienced a trauma because there is a certain amount of time that needs to pass to allow the brain to process and reconcile the thoughts and emotions. It may be that what seems like a traumatic event to the observer is actually dealt with by the victim as just another event in his life.

What is important to know is that longer term, no matter what the cause, there is always something that can be done to remove the trauma. The belief that someone has to find a way to live with it simply isn't true, in my opinion.

What About the Other 10%?

We know there is a battle going on in your head at all times between the subconscious, driven by The Caveman Rules, and the rational, controlled thought that sits in the prefrontal cortex. This logical part, let's call it conscious thought, is a behaviour regulator. It often overrides the primitive drives initiated by your subconscious. It's the part that distinguishes our behaviour from that of animals. For example, without the prefrontal cortex you would eat anything and everything that was available to the point of making yourself sick. You wouldn't store food. You would not be so interested in wearing clothes, and you would not be so restrained about satisfying your sexual urges! The prefrontal cortex helps us be human.

However, it has an awkward relationship with our subconscious. When focussed on survival, we can't afford to apply reason and take time to make decisions. Our survival is based on instant action and "gut instinct". With each instinctive survival response, there is both an emotional response, and a physiological response, that happens far quicker than conscious thought could ever drive. Given that our subconscious, the instant part of the brain, is in charge 90% of the day, it's some kind of miracle that we don't spend all day eating until we're sick and satisfying our primitive urges. But we don't, so what is it that makes the difference?

What is really easy to overlook is the fact that The Caveman Rules are here to protect us. That is how we are designed to work, so all being equal we do a pretty good job of getting on with our day-to-day lives despite them. It is only when one of the cavemen rules is inappropriately triggered that it begins to get in the way of our ability to have a happy life. Even so, in the main we survive very well. It's just happiness that is affected, not safety.

We can function perfectly well on autopilot as long as nothing is perceived as a threat. The decision to make a cup of coffee may require willpower to get up from where you are sitting, but most of us will actually go through the steps to make a cup of coffee without giving it any thought. Then one day, after almost no sleep, you find that this semi-automatic process, which you normally execute in a trance state, goes wrong. Maybe you forget to put water in the coffee machine or pour cold water into your cup instead of hot. In that moment, your attention is brought back to the steps you are taking, and you have to consciously think about your actions.

So what do we do with the other 10% while our subconscious looks after the automatic stuff? We think. We analyse. We make decisions. We take action. In fact, with the other 10% we do what we want to do, not what we need to do. That other 10% gives us the freedom to choose how to live our lives.

It is assumed that hearing multiple voices in your head is a bad thing, but we all do it. There is a constant dialogue going on between the conscious and subconscious parts. Which one wins is a result of a number of different factors.

Let's assume your subconscious is ticking over, getting on with the business of pumping blood round your body, breathing, fighting viruses and all those other automatic functions. There are no caveman rules active. You are now thinking using your conscious brain. Your pre-frontal cortex is fully engaged, and you are making choices that you want to make rather than those you have to make. This should mean you can get anything done that you want, but I'm sure you realise that isn't true. You know that pile of paperwork that you've been meaning to sort through? Somehow anything else, including scrubbing the cupboard out with a toothbrush, seems more appealing. Or how often do you find you get to the end of the day and you have no energy left to complete all the things you'd planned to do?

It's all about willpower and self-control. At the end of the day, the subconscious can always trigger off a response, but you have a choice to override that with rational conscious thought – a choice that requires willpower.

So let's say there is no virtual sabre-toothed tiger around and there is something challenging you that requires self-control. For example, you have walked past a bakery, and there is a lovely cake in the window that clearly has your name on it. What goes on? Without the prefrontal cortex it would be simple: want cake, eat cake. Your subconscious even gets your body ready (physiological reaction) by lowering your blood sugar ready for the spike it's about to get. However we do have a pre-frontal cortex, so the process is a bit more complex. The amount of self-control you are able to exert at this point is dependent on many factors:

1. Is the cake a sabre-toothed tiger? This is one of those situations that my clients beat themselves up over all the time. Something happens, and even though a part of them doesn't want the cake, a bigger part takes them into the shop and buys it. Afterwards, when the moment has passed, they can't get their head round why they didn't just resist it and walk on by. What happens is the equivalent of your head saying, "Oh look a shiny thing!", and while you are distracted trying to find the shiny thing, your head takes you in, buys the cake, eats the cake and tries to look all innocent when you look back again, having now realised there is no shiny thing. You stand there saying to yourself, "I can't believe I fell for that again!", but you have no choice. You are not consciously in control of your actions. Let's put it in a different context. If you believed that by not eating the cake then you were going to die, would you eat the cake? Usually the answer will be yes, of course. You'd be crazy not to eat the cake if the alternative was death. Well, that's what your subconscious believes.

2. Are you hungry or are you tired? If your blood sugar was already low and your subconscious has lowered it further in anticipation of the cake, then you have effectively now disabled your pre-frontal cortex. You are in survival mode. You no longer have free choice and you will buy the cake. I like to joke that your brain needs chocolate to think because it actually burns calories to use the pre-frontal cortex. If your blood sugar is okay you can think; if not you are surviving, and we all know how that plays out, don't we? This is also why you are less likely to be able to resist temptation if you are tired. All energy is routed into those functions that are critical for survival. Thinking is not one of those critical functions, unfortunately. So, if you are not hungry and you are not tired, then you have a pretty good chance of choosing not to eat the cake.

3. Is it later in the day? For the sake of illustration, imagine that each day you start with a container full of willpower points. As you go through the day you spend those points to get stuff done. The more you don't want to do something, the more points it will cost you. The more you are battling your subconscious to get something done, the more points it will cost you. So if you walk past the cake shop first thing in the morning, you are more likely to be able to keep walking because you still have some points in your container. However, if you have made the effort to go to the gym in the morning (and spent some of your willpower points) then head past the shop in the afternoon, you are more likely to be all out of points and go in. Have you ever noticed how much harder it is to get stuff done, or resist temptation, at the end of the day? This is because at the end of the day your container is likely to be at its lowest level of willpower points.

Increasing Your Willpower and Self-control

So is it possible to improve your willpower and self-control? Yes, it is. If you look again at the three things that affect willpower:

Challenge Number 1: It costs you more willpower points because you are battling your subconscious.

This is a therapy thing. You would need to get rid of the Thing to free you up from the "look a shiny thing!" moment. As you read through the ideas for increasing your self-control, be aware that they all still require that you exert choice, and if your subconscious equates the "thing" that is challenging your willpower to a sabre-toothed tiger, then you may not have enough willpower points to override that, even if your container is full!

Challenge Number 2: You are hungry or tired.

This is purely a factor of your physical state. If you are tired or hungry all bets are off. Don't beat yourself up over it – it is basic survival! I find I talk to a lot of mothers who are constantly berating themselves for not getting stuff done. They forget that they are not getting a decent night's sleep. They forget that before they were a mother, they were able to get stuff done without thinking about it. They see it as a sign of failure and a sign that something is going wrong in their head, that they can no longer think straight, where in reality it's simply that they are in survival mode out of necessity. When you are tired your prefrontal cortex does not have the energy it needs to function, and so you are almost entirely dependent on your subconscious – your 90%.

Challenge Number 3: You've already spent most of your willpower points.

The good news is that you can actually train your pre-frontal cortex like you would train any muscle in your body. By training it you can actually increase the size of the imaginary container that holds your willpower points. This means you start the day with more willpower points, which means you are more likely to have plenty available when you need them, no matter what time of day it is.

How do you train it up? Let's keep with the idea of being able to walk past the bakery as a case study. The goal here is to train your prefrontal cortex in such a way that you can start the day with a bigger container for your willpower points. The bigger the container, the more points you start the day with, the more likely there are points available to spend when you need to exert self-control.

Step 1: Taking Control

It doesn't matter what you do, as long as you do something that exerts a level of control over something that seems out of control. The action needs to be really specific, so you are taking decisive action. In our cake example you wouldn't want to say you are just trying to eat less sweet stuff. More specifically, your challenge is to stop eating cakes, so you need to do something to exert control over this. You need to start small. Tell yourself it's okay to buy the cake, but you will leave it thirty minutes before you eat it. Or you could buy the cake, but in order to eat it you must first cut it into four pieces. Or you could even eat it with your non-dominant hand because that requires concentration and control (i.e., your left hand if you are right-handed).

You might be amazed at how powerful taking a small amount of control can be. There are people who have given up smoking by only allowing themselves to smoke with their non-dominant hand or by allowing themselves to smoke only a brand they don't particularly like.

As you do something each day to take control, you might find that you can do more and more. You could get to the stage where you say you will have the cake but that you must walk past the shop and round the block before you go in. Eventually, you might surprise yourself when you realise how much easier it has become to just walk past the bakery and choose not to have the cake at all.

Step 2: Goals Versus Process

One of the conversations I often have with my coaching clients is, "What would you do if you won £10 million on the lottery?" Inevitably they say things like: pay off debts, treat family and friends, buy a big house, get a shiny car or five, have a holiday in the sun, etc. Then I ask, "And what will you be doing in ten years' time?" They tend to go quiet at that point.

You see, being goal-focussed is all well and good, but what happens when you reach the goal? Have you ever given it any thought? Have you thought about what will fill the void left behind once you have no goal? How about what will happen when you miss your goal? After all, sometimes there are circumstances outside of your control. How does it make you feel when you think about missing your goal? Does it give you licence to go wild and give up on everything?

The pressure of meeting a goal can provide one of the best excuses for giving in to something that is challenging your willpower. I'm sure we've all been there: "Oh it's too late now; I may as well go the whole hog and enjoy myself!" In the example with the cake, having a goal to not eat any cakes means that at any point, for the rest of your life, if you eat a cake then you have failed your goal. As a result, when you go into the bakery and buy the cake, you might decide you may as well make the most of missing your goal and buy a few more cakes while you are there. You then eat all the cakes you bought and feel terrible. You may then decide that you've now blown the whole week, so you may as well do the same thing the next day and the day after.

What if you were to change your willpower challenge from a goal to an aspiration? Instead of a hard and fast point that you need to reach, instead think of it more like a beacon somewhere up in the sky that you are aiming for. After all, never eating a cake again is not realistic, nor should it be really. Becoming fitter and healthier by cutting down on sweet things and cakes is realistic. If you are aiming for a bigger goal of being fitter and healthier, then each time you resist the cake you are heading in the right direction. More importantly, each time you eat a cake you are not failing at anything; you are just not taking a step any closer to where you want to go. You are focussed on the process rather than the goal, which means there is no such thing as failure and no excuse to beat yourself up. This different way of setting goals also helps you avoid that common trap of borrowing something from your future self. You know the one: "I will start going to the gym tomorrow," or "I was going to start the diet today, but instead I will start it on Monday." The thing about your willpower points is they start from fresh every day. You can't save them up and spend them the next day. When you go to bed the container is emptied. When you start the day it's full. So you can't borrow from, or bank and store for, tomorrow. Can you imagine how cross you would be if you woke up one day to find the previous day's version of you had already stolen half your willpower points?

Let's go back to the question I ask my clients. What would you do if you won £10 million on the lottery? Let's change it a little. If you win £10 million on the lottery, what will you be doing in ten years' time? When you track it back, the limitations on what people really want to do is rarely purely financial. It is mostly about belief. Having a bigger purpose rather than specific goals is a great way to align your conscious and subconscious on a common direction. When you face a choice of whether to give in to a primal need to survive or exert self-control and make a choice that is better for you and your future, having a beacon to aim for can make all the difference.

Step 3: Using Your Drugs Wisely

Our inability to exert willpower and self-control is not purely a matter of the thoughts and feelings that motivate us. The brain is a tricky thing. In the same way as your subconscious uses emotions to take control, your brain also uses drugs to make you behave in certain ways. We are all basically drug addicts without even realising it. Have you ever talked to someone who talks about the buzz they get from a good workout at the gym? If you are anything like me, you look at them like they are talking a foreign language! Seriously? Getting hot and sweaty and out of breath can be a good thing? Then I started running. I hate running. I am just not cut out for it. What I do love is the feeling afterwards – a sense of achievement. I also discovered that going for a run was way more revitalising than having a nap when I'd had a bad night's sleep.

This is all down to drugs. When you exercise, your brain releases endorphins. Endorphins are a feel-good chemical that interact with the neuro-receptors in your body. The feeling you get when endorphins are released is often compared to morphine. The advantage of endorphins over morphine, or other drugs, is that they are natural so have no negative side effects.

When your brain releases endorphins you find you can get stuff done. Endorphins actually make the container for your willpower points bigger. So if you are struggling with motivation, instead of trying to shut down to recharge your batteries, get out there; go for a walk or a run or even just walk up and down some stairs. Contrary to logic, because of the way endorphins work, doing more when you are tired actually gives you more energy, as opposed to using up your stock of energy. Of course, you also then get all the other marvellous benefits of doing more exercise too like benefits to your health and mental wellbeing. It's a bit of a win-win situation.

Ironically the biggest challenge to getting out there to release the endorphins can be motivation (i.e., willpower!). The more you do, the more you can do. So as with the cake scenario we went through, you can approach doing exercise in the same way. If you want to get to the gym then try getting started by just putting your gym kit on at the time of day you might have an opportunity. You don't actually have to believe you are going to go, but putting your kit on is taking action rather than giving in. For any willpower challenge it is possible to find a way to beat it one step at a time.

The other drug that plays a role in taking control is dopamine. I like to think of dopamine as the anticipation drug because it's a chemical that your brain releases in anticipation of getting something it recognises – something familiar. Once you get the thing that your brain is anticipating, the dopamine disappears and is replaced by either nothing or one of the other drugs like endorphins, serotonin or oxytocin. In fact it really doesn't matter whether the thing is a good or a bad thing, your brain will still release dopamine in anticipation of something it recognises. Experiments done on rats, where they could press a lever to stimulate dopamine release, showed that the rats would forgo basic needs of survival, such as food and water, in favour of getting the dopamine. Given the chance, the rats would become so obsessive about pressing the lever that they would starve instead of walking away from the "hit" for long enough to eat.

Like any drug, dopamine makes you feel good. So not getting dopamine makes you yearn for it. This is why as a human race we are so uncomfortable with change. It's why management consultancy companies make lots of money from working with corporations on change management programmes. It is also why it can be so hard to break a habit. When your brain doesn't recognise what you are doing, or about to do, it doesn't release dopamine. This makes you feel very uncomfortable without really understanding why. As a result you begin to look for logical reasons why you don't feel right. In work this can lead you to question the process or the management structure. When this is a habit like smoking, then it can lead you to find perfectly valid reasons why you should have a cigarette. You find the reasons to justify the feeling. When I work with clients on issues that they have had since childhood, they tend to go through a very uncomfortable time after our sessions because we have changed the thoughts in their head so much that they often don't recognise themselves any more. They don't recognise the way they respond to situations. The scale of change can be so uncomfortable that they almost yearn for the familiarity of the old thought patterns. They may have made them feel miserable, but at least it was a familiar misery!

The trick is to make the new thoughts and feelings as familiar as possible, as soon as possible. To do this, I use priming with my clients. It seems to be human nature to ignore the good stuff that has happened in the day in favour of the stuff you are not so happy with. If you are trying to lose weight and get up and go to the gym in the morning, and then in the afternoon you have some cake, you will almost definitely delete from your mind the fact you went to the gym and focus only on the fact that you had cake. You can prime yourself to notice the good stuff (and make the changes as familiar as possible as quickly as possible) by writing down three positive things that happened in your day at the end of every day. Let me explain why it's important to write it down.

Have you ever been in the process of buying a new car and

noticed that car everywhere? It's not that there are more of those cars on the roads; it's just that you have primed yourself to notice it. Have you ever been trying for a baby and found that everyone in the world is pregnant or has a baby? It's not true, it's just that you have primed yourself to notice it. By writing your positives down at the end of the day, you have to notice the good stuff that is always there, and because you are writing them down, you can't delete them from memory. Also, because your brain knows you need to write down three things at the end of the day, it will go looking for them. You are priming yourself to see the good stuff.

It doesn't have to be big things either. It can be someone making you smile, like noticing a bird singing in the morning. Good stuff is always there. The worse the day is, the more effort you should make to write them down. It can make the difference between a good and a bad day if you stick to it, and in the long run, it can ensure that when something is changing that you get dopamine for the new stuff as soon as possible. The good news is, you will also get the other good drugs that are associated with happiness like serotonin and oxytocin.

Going back to our case study on the cake, the anticipation of eating the cake is way more powerful and stimulating than the actual taste of the cake itself. I'm sure you've had times where you have walked past a food place and been almost overwhelmed by the delicious smells, only to be disappointed by the actual flavour of the food. When you entertain the idea of having the cake, your brain releases dopamine in anticipation of having something that you want. Like all the other reasons to go and buy the cake weren't enough, you now have a chemical going through your body that makes you feel good just thinking about it! It's not fair really. You are no longer just battling a survival instinct; you are also battling a drug addiction. This is not an easy one to overcome. It's hard to turn your back on drugs. To beat this particular obstacle to exerting self-control, you have to accept that there will be a period of time where you are uncomfortable because you are going cold turkey. To overcome the drug addiction, become aware of that moment where the anticipation of something is becoming compelling, then label that feeling as a hit of drugs and ignore what it's compelling you to do. You can even say to yourself, "I will not be a drug addict." Dopamine is an anticipation drug. It doesn't care what you get at the end. In fact it cares so little that as soon as you have the thing that you were anticipating, the dopamine totally disappears. So it's meaningless. Like with the rat, it's the anticipation that inspires the action not the reward at the end.

Step 4: Just Breathe

It's funny, this breathing thing; it's something your subconscious manages all day, every day, without you having to give any thought to it at all. At the same time, you can take conscious control over your breathing, and by doing that, you can make all sorts of marvellous things happen in your body.

The best way of engaging the benefit of breathing is to practise some form of meditation or mindfulness. There have been many studies on the benefits of this lately. It is more and more becoming an accepted practice in improving mental and physical health (rather than something quirky practised by hippies and Buddhist monks!). I always think mindfulness is a weird description actually. I think body-fullness would be far more accurate as it describes what you are actually trying to do. The idea is to spend at least ten minutes a day focussing on nothing other than your breathing. You can accept that thoughts will come and go. There are a number of different ways of dealing with this, depending on who you talk to, but in a nutshell, your intent should be to not allow the thoughts to sit in your head. Instead, keep your focus on each breath in and each breath out and let the thoughts drift off again once they appear. Personally I find this almost impossible, but I really understand the principle of how this can lead to an increase in focus, and as a result, a bigger container for your willpower points.

If you remember, early on in this book I talked about *The Wonderful Story of Henry Sugar* by Roald Dahl. The ability to focus on the candle enhanced the ability to focus overall. This exercise would be useful in training up the pre-frontal cortex. I personally have found that the only way I can focus on anything is to fill my mind with as many things as I can to the point where a small part of it is able to truly focus. To write this book, I am doing at least three other things on my computer at the same time. It's the way I work.

Everyone will have her own way of practising mindfulness, and I could quote thousands of studies in here, but as I said at the start, that's not what this book is about. You can look it up yourself. (See some of the books referenced in the bibliography.) Suffice to say, if you want to increase the size of the container that holds your willpower points at the start of the day, then just spending a few minutes every day in some sort of mindfulness practice is a pretty easy way to achieve that.

Practical Steps to Taking More Control

In summary:

1. Identify the biggest challenge to your willpower.

2. Do one thing each day to take control over your subconscious.

3. Identify your long term "big picture" goal for beating your willpower.

4. What would the "you" in the future think of the "you" now borrowing from them?

5. Are you getting a dopamine hit?

6. Get rid of excuses by asking, "Is that really true?" For example, "I can't get to the gym because I don't have time."

7. Spend time every day just breathing.

So What?

Many years ago, when I was a business consultant, I was delivering a presentation to a senior manager in a large organisation. I had pretty charts and slides to show him how the speed of work had improved while the number of incidents had reduced. It was good stuff, and I was feeling quite proud of my lovely colourful charts and graphs. That is, I was until he looked at me and said, "So what?"

So what? I had done all this work and was expecting "woo hoo", not "so what?"

He explained that he wanted to know what it meant to the customer. As it happened, the customers were still unhappy because the stuff I was talking about didn't really measure what affected them.

Ever since then, "so what?" is a question I often ask myself to check whether I am looking at something in the right way. I even ask my clients (although I usually make the phrasing of the question a little less direct!).

Client: "I want to lose weight and get down to a size 10."
Me: "What would it matter if you stayed at the size you are now for the rest of your life?"

Client: "I can't stop worrying about the future."
Me: "How does worrying about the future all the time actually cause you a problem?"

Client: "I want to stop eating chocolate."
Me: "What's wrong with eating chocolate?"

If you were to ask "so what?" about The Caveman Rules, then it might be quite difficult to see them as anything other than a bad thing. However, there is actually some merit in the rules. They have helped us survive this long after all. So let's go back and look at them again but this time in a different way. Let us now ask what value there might be in still following a particular rule.

Rule 1 – React First or You'll Die.

If you think about it, there are many things it is good to be nervous about or even scared of. Without a fear of heights you might take unnecessary risks. A fear of dangerous critters like snakes forces you to keep your distance. In these circumstances it is very healthy, and key to your survival, to exercise caution. The physical response triggered by your subconscious increases your chance of survival. If we lost this rule altogether the survival of the race would be at risk. What we actually need to do is to stop equating emotional hurt to physical hurt. They are simply not the same level of risk and don't belong together in this rule.

Rule 2 – If Your Parents Don't Love You, You'll Die.

Love is fundamental to being human. Love is not an easy thing to learn about, but it's love that is responsible for survival of the race, especially as more and more of the world develops and moves on from arranged marriage. Once you have the freedom to choose your partner, it is love, rather than tradition, that becomes the key to survival. When you have a child, love is the thing that makes you care for them. Love keeps you alive and keeps the race alive. As a child you have to learn about love somehow, and it's such a complex concept that, to some degree, it has to be distilled into something more black and white. As you grow up you need to be able to watch, understand, and learn emotional connections. The problem is that the execution of this rule leads to things being connected to love that had nothing to do with it. In an attempt to understand love, the subconscious connects things to love incorrectly. Somehow we need to end up where we can understand what love is, while at the same time being able to accept that love is not about actions but about belief. Good luck working out a rule for that one!

Rule 3 – If You Are Not Part of a Pack You'll Die.

"The whole is greater than the sum of its parts." Have you heard that phrase? It means that if you combine things into one as a cohesive unit, then it is greater than adding up the individual strengths of the parts. It is not true anymore that if you are not part of a pack then you will die. However it is true that by working as a team you can achieve so much more. This is especially true if you leverage each other's strengths. What we need to lose is the belief that if you don't fit in, then you are not good enough – that you are weak. What we need to keep is the belief that more can be achieved when working together in a social group.

Maybe now you can see that the problem is not as much with the rules, as with the interpretation and execution of them in our modern, evolved society. The problem is that the rules need to evolve. So far they have adapted (to include emotional measures) but not evolved (changed in their execution).

If your brain is working on an outdated set of rules, where are they stored, and why has evolution not changed them?

Let's start by looking at the topic of nature versus nurture. Someone comes to see me who has low self-worth because of Rule Number 3: If you are not part of a pack you will die. He was bullied at school and has had social anxiety ever since. He protects his children from it because he assumes the same will happen to them. There is a strong component of nature versus nurture here. Nature says if you are singled out as different then you are weak. If you are weak you can't survive. Nature also says you need to adopt the beliefs and values of your parents so that you earn their love (according to Caveman Rule Number 2). Nurture says a mother and father will protect their children from the experiences they struggled with. You could argue that the child of a bullied parent is going to have a really tough time! I can help get rid of the problem in the parent so that they are not so over-protective, but I can't change the nature of someone.

Think about families with more than one child. Each child is unique. Even with twins or triplets, each child will have its own unique personality. One might be outgoing and confident. Another might prefer being on her own. One might enjoy the limelight whilst the other shies away from it. This is not nurture. We are born with these personality traits. People are often surprised at how different brothers and sisters can be, as if there is an expectation that they will be the same as their parents. Whilst this is often true for appearance, it is rarely true for personality – the stuff that is in the head. I don't believe nurture defines who we are, but I do believe that through nurture we can mess someone up!

I am uncomfortable in social situations. I choose to sit in the back of the room rather than at the front when I go to events. When I go to networking meetings, I always mess up on the key bit where you go and talk to people by trying to be invisible in the corner. However, if I get a chance to stand on a stage and talk to people, I am in my element. I couldn't be happier. I love the buzz I get from talking to people and training people. I love communicating. I write all the time. I blog all the time. I am on Twitter all the time. I love people. You might think from the first part of this description that I am an introvert, but really I am a closet extrovert. My mood is seriously affected by a lack of human contact. All it takes is one conversation over a beer or a cup of coffee, and I have enough ideas and energy to keep me going for a week. I am actually a pretty poor version of an introvert. An introvert is someone who is drained of energy by being around people. An extrovert is someone who gets more energy from being around people.

Things changed for me as I had therapy. I realised that those things that I believed were innate to my personality, like being uncomfortable around people and avoiding getting close to people, were actually a survival technique. Because of what I went through in my childhood, I learnt to lay low and avoid contact. Every social situation was more a risk to be endured rather than an opportunity to connect. Then one day I realised that I no longer jumped when someone casually placed a hand on my arm. It was a revelation to me because I didn't realise it made me jump until it didn't anymore! After that I realised that I was actually comfortable in social situations. I felt okay sitting in a packed carriage on the London Underground. Again, I hadn't even realised I was uncomfortable until I no longer was.

My nature is to be okay in social situations. My nature is to enjoy the company of others and to get energised by discussion and communication. Nurture messed that up for me. Nurture made those things risky and uncomfortable. Nature defines us. Nurture messes us up. Nature holds The Caveman Rules. We know these rules are passed down between generations. What we don't know is how.

What I do know is that the rules used by our subconscious to drive our behaviour day in, day out, have not changed since the caveman days. However, the execution of them has adapted slightly to apply to modern day situations:

Rule 1: It doesn't matter whether the thing that hurts you is physical or emotional; your subconscious still thinks it's the equivalent of a sabre-toothed tiger and triggers the same response as if you had to fight, run away or freeze. This applies equally to something that doesn't physically threaten you, like public speaking, and to something where there is a genuine risk, like going up to a high place. The subconscious does not discriminate in its response.

Rule 2: The fundamental belief of your subconscious is that if, for whatever reason, you are not loved, then this will mean you don't get fed and cared for, and you will die. It is irrelevant that in modern society a lack of love does not equal a lack of food and care. This rule also now applies to any responsible adult, not just your mother.

Rule 3: It also believes that the best chance of survival is to be in a pack and that failure to be accepted by the pack equates to almost certain death. Measures of "fitting in" now include wearing the right clothes, having the right hairstyle, or countless other things that are, in reality, no indication of strength or weakness.

Our subconscious has not fully adapted and changed. Isn't that weird? Where evolution teaches us that species must adapt or die, in this area we have barely adapted, and yet we have still survived. Other things have changed, including the full development of a prefrontal cortex, walking on two legs, and other more subtle changes. Yet the rules remain.

Let's look at a couple of ways things are passed down genetically, in an attempt to understand how The Caveman Rules are transferred.

In the DNA

I have a pretty simple way of looking at things. Let's consider a car. To manufacture a car you need a blueprint. The blueprint details the instructions on how to put the car together. The body is constructed, in part, using the genetic encoding held within the DNA. The DNA holds the blueprint for the body.

With each new generation of car the blueprint is updated to make the car more efficient, give it extra functionality, or even make it look nicer. If you want to update the car, then you need to first update the blueprint. With a blueprint there is a person, or a group of people, responsible for assessing the performance of the car and making decisions about the changes that are needed.

With the DNA there is no single person making decisions about how it should be changed. The update happens over time when enough evidence has been gathered to show a change is necessary. Changes to DNA are not made on a whim to "try it out"; they are made when the chances of survival will be enhanced by the change. They are a result of learned behaviour and experience. Those animals that fail to adapt die out. Those that adapt survive. The changes tend to be to our physical qualities: standing upright, a bigger pre-frontal cortex, etc. Changes don't appear to happen in the brain in the same way (although because so little is known about how the brain works, it is entirely feasible that there have been very significant changes through evolution!).

Once the car has been manufactured, the blueprint serves no real purpose. In a similar way, up until recently, it was believed that the DNA was used to grow the cells, etc., but served no ongoing purpose. Opinions are changing now as more is understood through research into epigenetics. It appears there are genetic switches inherent in the DNA that can actually be turned on and off midway through our lifespan.

So we know there have been countless physical changes as we've evolved, but what about changes in the way we think? It's hard to know for sure because we are still quite ignorant on the workings of the brain. However, it is clear that we are still following caveman rules in many areas, which suggests a lack of change in our cognitive process despite the expansion in our cognitive ability. It also suggests that things like memories and emotional responses may not be stored in our DNA, because if they were, then surely they would have evolved in the same way as our physical attributes?

There is a lot of research going on right now into the field of Epigenetics.

I pulled the following definition from www. livescience.com:

Epigenetics literally means "above" or "on top of" genetics. It refers to external modifications to DNA that turn genes "on" or "off". These modifications do not change the DNA sequence, but instead, they affect how cells "read" genes.

Amazingly we still don't understand much about the body in terms of what governs behaviour, and most people vastly underestimate the mind/body connection. As we learn more, people are beginning to see that the solution to some of genetic diseases may be a shift in the genetic coding, rather than symptom treatment.

Let's go back to the story of the mouse. (Poor mice, they get a rough ride!) The following is an extract from *The Telegraph* newspaper. In his article, 'Phobias May Be Memories Passed Down in Genes from Ancestors', Richard Gray writes:

In a study, which is published in the journal *Nature Neuroscience*, the researchers trained mice to fear the smell of cherry blossom using electric shocks before allowing them to breed.

The offspring produced showed fearful responses to the odour of cherry blossom compared to a neutral odour, despite never having encountered them before.

This suggests it is possible to implant a phobia. If the DNA is the blueprint that is updated through evolution, then a single generation is not enough time to validate the need for a blueprint change. The association between the smell of cherry blossom and an electric shock needs to be stored elsewhere, or possibly triggered by a genetic switch. Either way, given that DNA takes generations to change, it is unlikely, in my opinion, that The Caveman Rules are stored in the DNA sequence.

In the Cells

So the blueprint is used to manufacture the car, but the car is useless without a driver. It doesn't matter how many bells and whistles it has, without someone to operate them, it is just a useless hunk of metal and plastic. Without the brain, the body has no driver. Without the body, the brain has nothing to do. A car is useless without a driver. A driver has no purpose without a car.

So what does this mean to the whole evolution discussion? Well, you can change a car as much as you want, but if you don't change the driver, or the driver doesn't change, you probably won't get the best out of it. Some of the fundamentals will always remain the same, but to really appreciate any changes as the car is upgraded, you need to know how to use them. And because the car is nothing without a driver, then some of the coolest features may remain unused if the driver is stuck in their ways.

The brain is the driver. The body is the car. Our bodies have evolved in amazing ways, but the brain has barely moved. It has changed enough to function in modern society, but not enough to make full use of the benefits of evolution.

To the driver, the blueprint is useless. The driver interacts with the wheel, the pedals and the gears. The driver has a destination and interacts with the car to reach the destination.

To the brain, the DNA doesn't really serve any purpose. The brain interacts with the cells and organs in the body to achieve what it needs. Some of it is automatic: the heart beating, breathing, immune response, etc. Even that is still controlled by the brain; it's just outside of our conscious awareness. All you need to do is to focus on your breathing to realise how strong the mind/body connection is. Breathe faster or breathe slower, and you will feel your heart rate speed up or slow down. You are using conscious choice to change the behaviour of your body.

Some stuff happens semi-automatically like walking. Walking is a partnership between conscious and subconscious thought. If you've ever had an injury in your leg, then you will have had the chance to experience what happens when the balance of that partnership changes. It's also something you can see when you are tired. There are things that usually require little focus, but when you are tired, those same things can seem like you have to put in loads of effort. This is because the conscious mind needs energy to function, and when you are tired, it doesn't have enough. When the conscious mind doesn't have the energy to function, it takes a back seat to the subconscious – to automatic functions.

Some stuff is totally a result of conscious thought, like going for a run. You can reach a level of unconscious competence, but you need to actively decide to increase your pace to a run, keep running until you have covered sufficient distance or time, what speed you will run, etc.

So how does the body respond to the brain? What is the channel of communication between the brain and the body? For a car it is clear. Each action by the driver engages gears and electrical circuits to deliver a specific response. It is not so clear for the mind and body.

A friend once said, "What the mind believes the body achieves." Did you know that it is possible to train up a muscle in your body by just repeating a motion in your head over and over again, in the same way that you would physically practise? A sports person can rehearse a move like a golf swing or shooting a hoop even more effectively by only doing it in their head because they can be more consistent. Isn't that amazing? Just by thinking your way through something you can physically change your body.

If you think about it, that's all we are saying with Caveman Rule Number 1. In response to a threat perceived by the head, a set of physical reactions are triggered in the body. You can also change the mind by changing a physical reaction (e.g., by using simple breathing techniques). Mind and body inform each other all the time.

In his book, *The Biology of Belief*, Bruce Lipton explains about cells and how they behave. I found it fascinating in the context of genetic memories – fascinating because he talks about the way we believe – that the nucleus of a cell is the brain of the cell. However, apparently you can kill off the nucleus, but the cell still survives for a couple of weeks. Yet if you do anything to damage the membrane around the outside of a cell, then the cell will die straight away. The membrane is the communication conduit. It takes instructions from the environment and passes them into the cell, which then uses its programming (probably in DNA) to take action. It's the environment of the cell that really dictates how the cell behaves. What is the environment for the cells that live in the human body? What directs the physical responses of the body in response to external factors? What keeps the body ticking? The brain. And because this all happens automatically, it is the subconscious that is the real driver.

In an article on the Human Genome Project, Lipton writes:

One of the perennial controversies that tends to evoke rancor among biomedical scientists concerns the role of nature versus nurture in the unfoldment of life [Lipton, 1998a]. Those polarized on the side of nature invoke the concept of genetic determinism as the mechanism responsible for "controlling" the expression of an organism's physical and behavioral traits. Genetic determinism refers to an internal control mechanism resembling a genetically-coded "computer" program. At conception, it is believed that the differential activation of selected maternal and paternal genes collectively "download" an individual's physiologic and behavioral character, in other words, their biological destiny.

The subconscious drives the body by communicating with the cell membrane to guide cell behaviour. This is why, often, when a doctor (or anyone who is perceived as an authority figure) gives you a diagnosis, you will believe it unquestioningly. If a doctor tells you that you have three months to live, then most people will live for a maximum of three months. Those who refuse to accept a diagnosis, and instead choose to pursue their own path to healing, often well outlive the medical predications.

Let's go back to the car. The car is manufactured from a blueprint, and the body is made from the DNA. The car needs a driver to operate it. The body is operated by the brain, and more specifically the subconscious. The driver engages with specific parts of the car to operate it and to communicate with the engine (the accelerator, brake pedal, etc.). The brain engages with the body via the cells. Communication with the cells is through the cell membrane.

Almost every day studies are coming out showing there is a measurable connection between the mind and body. The difference in health between happy and angry people and even the health benefits of a hug (apparently it needs to be at least twenty seconds long to get some benefit) have been measured scientifically. Every time I read one of these studies my mind is opened further to the possibilities.

If we go with the theory that genetic memories are held in the cells, then it is possible that the cell membrane holds these memories. This means when cells combine in the womb to produce a new life, this is how The Caveman Rules (and person-alised variants) are passed on to the next generation. This would certainly explain how it was possible to pass down a phobia in a single generation with the mouse. Maybe The Caveman Rules and other learned behaviours are actually transferred via the cell membrane? It's also possible that the cell membrane activates or deactivates some sort of genetic switch in the DNA held inside the cell.

Some Other Way?

Maybe it is all in the head? Maybe it is all stored in the brain in some way. After all, we barely understand even a fraction of how the brain works. Increasingly we are beginning to appreciate the true power of our thoughts over our physical well-being – but appreciating is not the same as fully understanding!

The problem with thoughts and anything that happens in the head is that they are intangible. You can't see a thought. You can't stick a bandage on something that is emotionally painful. You can't scratch a niggling negative thought. So how do you change something in the head? The answer is obvious: you make it tangible. In Neuro Linguistic Programming (NLP), this is used a lot.

Let's look at pain as a great example of this. Difficult though it is to believe, pain doesn't actually happen at the source (like a broken bone or a cut). The first thing to happen, on detection of a problem, is a signal is sent to the brain saying, "Hi boss, there is this thing going on; how should I respond?" The brain then makes a judgement call on what level the pain should be. Do you need to turn the pain up because something is on your foot and you need to get it off? Or is it something that doesn't require immediate attention, so the pain doesn't need to be too high? Do you need to continue doing what you are doing for the sake of survival? In this case you need the pain to stay away until you are safe. The brain then sends instructions back to the source to tell it what to do.

We've all heard of those situations where someone was able to do amazing feats despite terrible injuries. The adrenalin surging through our body is designed to help us survive against the odds. It also works against us. If you are in pain and are bored, then there is nothing to distract you, and because your brain can focus on the pain, it often feels worse. There is also the concept of low and high pain thresholds. Pain is subjective and individual because it is the result of an interpretation made in the brain.

What this means is that, potentially, we can control pain with our mind. Let's take a headache. A simple headache is a pain in the head without any obvious physical cause. Next time you have a headache, follow the steps bellow:

1. You need to make the pain tangible, so close your eyes and imagine that the pain has a colour. It can be any colour, whichever one first springs to mind. We know the subconscious doesn't take time to think, so whatever comes to mind first is what you should use.

2. If that colour was in some sort of shape, what would it be? Spend a few moments thinking about the shape. Is it 2D or 3D? Is it shiny or matt? Does it have a temperature? Is it moving? Is it making a sound?

3. Now that we have imagined the pain as an object, we can change the object and change the pain. What can you do to that shape to make it less powerful? The answer to this may be obvious. If not here are some options:

   • Can you change the shape until you can't make it out any more? This may be through shrinking it, dissolving it, throwing it away, or something else.

   • If it has spiky or sharp edges, can you make them blunt by either changing the material to something softer or squashing them down? I had one client who saw brambles and made the spikes into rubber then flattened them off. Another client felt her back pain as a sword down her spine. She just turned it to jelly. You might want to dissolve the shape or even just throw it away.

   • If it is vibrating or making a noise, can you change the speed of the vibration or the pitch of the noise?

- If you are not changing the object to get rid of it, you might find you need to change the colour too.

When you open your eyes you might be surprised to find the pain has gone. You changed something that felt physical by changing your thoughts. This is a very small scale example of how simple it is to change thoughts and affect your body by changing your thoughts. Imagine the possibilities this could open up in your life!

So What?

Irrespective of how they are passed down, we know the following about The Caveman Rules of Survival:

1. They are passed down from generation to generation with little evidence of evolutionary change.

2. It is theoretically possible to pass a learned rule down to the next generation.

3. Whilst the rules have a role in our survival, they are outdated, and there is little sign of that changing in generations to come.

In the absence of any answers, having an awareness of where your thoughts and behaviours come from gives you the means to begin the process of change.

Your subconscious means well. It's just a bit jumpy and oversensitive. Around every corner it believes there is the possibility of death, and it wants to keep you safe. By understanding this, you can acknowledge and accept the positive intent of your subconscious and utilise that precious 10% to focus and take control.

You can make the choices you want to live the life you want.

Books That Inspired Me

Maximum Willpower: How to Master the New Science of Self-Control,
   Kelly McGonigal
Monsters and Magical Sticks, Stephen Heller and Terry Steele
How Your Mind Can Heal Your Body, Dr David Hamilton
The Biology of Belief, Bruce Lipton
The Decisive Moment, Jonah Lehrer
Blink, Malcolm Gladwell
Cognitive Hypnotherapy: What's That About and How Can I Use It?,
   Trevor Silvester
*In an Unspoken Voice: How the Body Releases Trauma and Restores
   Goodness*, Peter A. Levine
When You're Falling, Dive: Using Your Pain to Transform Your Life,
   Mark Matousek
Molecules of Emotion: Why You Feel the Way You Feel, Deepak
   Chopra and Candace Pert
Love, Medicine and Miracles, Dr Bernie Siegel

Online Resources
**Reference to the mouse experiment (I originally read about it
in *New Scientist*):**
http://www.telegraph.co.uk/science/science-news/10486479/
Phobias-may-be-memories-passed-down-in-genes-from-
ancestors.html

Definition of Epigenetics
www.livescience.com

Jean Piaget: How a Child Thinks (YouTube)
https://www.youtube.com/watch?v=Jw33CBsEmR4

CHANGE
MAKERS
BOOKS

Changemakers publishes books for individuals committed to
transforming their lives and transforming the world. Our
readers seek to become positive, powerful agents of change.
Changemakers books inform, inspire, and provide practical
wisdom and skills to empower us to create the next chapter of
humanity's future.
Please visit our website at www.changemakers-books.com